My Food

For my wife, Mary, and my children Andre, Alice,
Eugenia and Stefanie Ruby
C.L.

For my singular parents, Thomas and Marjorie Steel,
and my loving family, John, Francesca and Sebastian
E.H.

My Food

Cheong Liew
with Elizabeth Ho

Illustrations by Timothy John

Foreword by Barbara Santich

ALLEN & UNWIN

About the artist

Timothy John has been associated with Cheong Liew from the early days of Neddy's, when he incorporated Cheong's saying 'Anything is possible' into his graphics for the restaurant. He was the obvious choice for illustrator when this book was first mooted, and his beautiful and distinctive work is a perfect expression of Cheong Liew's particular genius.

Born in Adelaide in 1958, Timothy John began to exhibit in 1980, and had his first solo exhibition at Bonython Meadmore Gallery in Adelaide in 1984. Since then, he has exhibited at least once a year, with shows in most Australian capitals as well as Himeji, Paris, New York and Havana.

Timothy John's work is held in major Australian public collections, and in private collections throughout Australia, USA, Asia and Europe.

© Cheong Liew & Elizabeth Ho 1995
Illustrations © Timothy John 1995

First published in 1995

Allen & Unwin Pty Ltd
9 Atchison Street
St Leonards NSW 2065, Australia

National Library of Australia
cataloguing-in-publication data:

Cheong, Liew
My food.

Bibliography.
Includes index.
ISBN 1 86373 739 1.

1. Cookery. I. Ho, Elizabeth F. (Elizabeth Francesca). II. Title.

641.5

Cover and text design by Cornwell Design
Printed in Australia by Southwood

10 9 8 7 6 5 4 3 2 1

Contents

Neddy's Classic   11

The seventies: nouvelle cuisine, nouvelle style, nouvelle ingredients, experimentation—even revolution—in technique and ingredients, the dare to eat this period at Neddy's.

Warm salad of Moreton Bay bugs with toasted salted fish *16*; Steamed cucumber and lambs' brains with spicy tomato sauce *19*; Tea-smoked quail, preserved eggs and glacé ginger in sweet pastry *21*; Timbale of jellied prawns and steamed pheasant with mustard green salad *24*; Spicy calamari with swamp cabbage and chilli hoi sin sauce *27*; Shark lips, scallops and sea cucumber braised in carrot oil *30*; Kangaroo fillet, veal tongue and braised witlof *34*; Roast suckling pig with green ginger wine and spiced spinach purée *36*; Anise and ginger flavoured duck with steamed lotus bun *38*; Rhubarb tart with clove cream and chocolate figs *40*; Black rice and palm sugar pudding *42*

Adelaide Courtyard   45

A summer courtyard in Adelaide recalled the Mediterranean, the Middle East, Asia, and the Australian back garden, inspiring food that reflected the multicultural mood of Australia.

Lamb Sahara with naan bread *48*; Orange and honeydew grenadine salad *50*; Garlic pâté with grilled bread *51*; Pot-roasted pigeon with garlic and grilled figs *53*; Grilled red mullet with lemon, chilli and marjoram *55*; Warm salad of shiitake and abalone mushrooms with pasta *57*; Cabbage salad with spiced sweet tomato dressing *60*; Cucumber and bitter green salad with lime dressing *61*; Deep-fried mussels in soft batter *62*; Kangaroo Moroccan style with couscous and chick peas *63*; White pork slices with garlic sauce *65*; Chinese shortcake served with jasmine tea *66*

Liew Family Gathering   69

The 'miss-most' food of the Liew family—flavours, aromas and combinations from the Malay Peninsula, where food traditions have been mixed for well over two hundred years.

Indian rojak *72*; Dingwu vegetarian platter *76*; Loquat mandolin-shaped duck *80*; Nonya-style korma chicken curry *82*; Black bean and chilli rice vermicelli

84; Mongolian-style deep-fried spiced goat 86; Grandma's fun kwor 88; Thai-style baked mulloway 90; Red-roast chicken salad with a chilli-oil vinaigrette 92; Stir-fried southern king prawns with asparagus and abalone mushrooms 94; Steamed eggplant with tomato chilli sauce 96; Fresh fruit tapioca pudding with palm sugar 98

Sunday Birthday Lunch Buffet   101

An innovative and celebratory menu that is informal and unpretentious but sophisticated.

Saffron fish consommé with salmon-roe cream and toasted shallot 104; Spicy fried calamari mughlai style with sweet fragrant rice 106; Olive-fried giant southern octopus and avocado salad 109; Deep-fried brandade cubes with elephant eyes 112; Nanjing salad 115; Nonya chilli mud crab 117; Peking-style roast duck wrapped in lotus pancake 119; Braised lamb neck with beef tendon 122; Orange and Grand Marnier soufflé cake 124

Simple Chinese Home Menu   127

Hidden Chinese treasures balancing elements and ingredients and introducing some basic but essential techniques; traditional fresh ingredients are the key to success, as they are for all truly great cuisines.

Steamed Atlantic salmon fillet with spring onions and fresh coriander 131; Perfect steeped white chicken 133; Red-roast callop with greens, spring onion and coriander sauce 135; Green choy sum with white-bait stock 138; Lamb or goat casserole with red dates, water chestnuts and wood fungus 139; Crisp stuffed eggplant salad 141; Steamed jasmine-scented white rice 143; Red bean paste pancakes 144

Let the Dance Begin   147

Flavour and texture, richness and contrast—this is not a menu for the faint-hearted, but why not try your hand? Cheong pushes back the boundaries with a menu of elegant complexity, created for the Adelaide Hilton, 1993.

Deep-fried oysters with garlic chives in bean-curd pastry 150; Chinese-style pickled raw fish with steamed mussels 152; Venison consommé with shark-fin pouch 154; Warm salad of pig's head with baby vegetables 157; Crisp spiced pigeon on snow-pea shoot risotto 160; Ragout of possum with root vegetables 163; Green salad 165; Caramelised pear napoleon with tea sorbet 166

Adelaide Extravaganza   171

Subtle, complex, daring and refined—new heights in cuisine for the adventurous.

Drunken chicken, jellyfish salad, 'smoked fish' and black-peppered pineapple 174; Slow-braised abalone, veal sweetbreads and black moss 177; Red-roast snapper with shaved cuttlefish and leek fondue 179; Loin of lamb with shahjira

Favourite Desserts   *203*

Influenced by traditional European dessert chefs and inspired by the spices and fruits of Asia, and the fresh produce of Australia.

Master Recipes   *219*

The fundamentals: master these skills and you have the foundation for innumerable exquisite dishes.

Glossary   *233*

Note

Metric units are used throughout the book. Conversions:

10 ml	0.352 fl oz		5 g	0.176 oz
30 ml	1 fl oz		10 g	0.353 oz
100 ml	3 fl oz		125 g	4 oz
150 ml	5 fl oz		250 g	8 oz
250 ml	8 fl oz		500 g	1 lb
500 ml	16 fl oz		1 kg	2 lb
1 litre	35 fl oz		*(Precise conversions in bold type)*	

Celsius	80	90	100	110	120	130	140	150	160	170	180	190	200	210	220	230	240	250
Fahrenheit	175	190	200		250		275	300	325		350	375	400		425	450		475

Mm	2	3	5	10	Cm	2.54	5	10	20	30	40	50
Inches	1/6	1/8	1/4	1/2	Inches	1	2	4	8	12	16	20

Acknowledgments

While we have thoroughly enjoyed this three-year journey called co-authorship, it would have been an impossible one without the support of our respective partners, Mary Ziukelis and John Ho; wise counsel from master chef Urs Inauen; the empathetic genius of our illustrator, Tim John; the gentle and perceptive guidance of our editor, now friend, Anna Dollard; and the encouragement of our first editor, Julie Gibbs.

We can honestly say that we have maintained our sense of harmony throughout. In collegiate spirit and friendship, we thank each other for lively conversations and shared determination.

Also to thank are the many people who have shaped our understanding of food and stimulated our interest in Australian cultural definition. Parents have been mentioned elsewhere, but special thanks go to Wan-Thye Liew and Cheong Sow Keng for their precious gift of knowledge in the Neddy's years. The connections are all there.

We acknowledge our publishers, Allen & Unwin, and all those people who make books happen. We thank Hilton International, especially Greg Huggett at the Adelaide Hilton, for promotional support.

Finally, we salute those Australians who put their hearts into creating quality produce, against the mass-produced tide, and those Australians who appreciate the difference and ask for it.

Preface

In all chapters except Favourite Desserts and Master Recipes, we have organised the dishes into menus consisting of entrées, main courses and one or two desserts. All recipes are designed for six people, but serves may be small or large, and most dishes that appear at the beginning of the menus are entrée size. Any dish can be adapted to serve as an entrée or main course.

We had a number of ideas when we were planning this book. One was to offer a 'language' of food, a way of describing the essential nature of a dish and its origins.

Another was to encourage a fresh spirit of interpretation, based on an understanding of origins, rather like a composer bringing out the best in all the instruments and creating new harmonies. We wanted to celebrate Australia's multicultural consciousness and an evolving sense of our own cuisine.

We also wanted to promote respect for basic ingredients, the fresh produce and spices that underpin each dish.

With these ideas in mind the recipes are introduced by both of us; Cheong's thoughts in italics, with further advice from Liz.

In this book there is a place for personal discovery, and readers should have the confidence to adapt and build on what is presented here—there is no such thing as 'only a home cook'. Therefore, while there may be guidance, there are no hard and fast rules about how you interpret the dishes. You can choose to serve dishes as main courses or entrées, or as an informal platter or buffet.

Similarly, the menu arrangement offers you, the chef, choices about what to omit or include. Each menu reflects a mood and a theme. If you are entertaining a large group you may wish to present every dish. If your time is limited you may adapt your favourites and make large platters. You may cater for small appetites at an intimate dinner party by choosing only the lighter dishes and serving them as a series of 'tastes'.

Be aware of your personal vision for a dish; this is more important than rigidly following a recipe. Your individual rhythm and style will always affect how a dish turns out.

We encourage you to use the repertoire of your senses, and to believe in your own power to create. Be our guest and be the judge!

Cheong Liew and Elizabeth Ho

Foreword

Barbara Santich

'Why do we eat?' ask Hsiang Ju Lin and Tsuifeng Lin, authors of *Chinese Gastronomy*. 'In order to pursue the flavour of things,' comes their ready response. Cheong Liew—Adelaide chef, teacher, restaurateur and, with Phillip Searle, creator of memorable banquets—*cooks* 'in order to pursue the flavour of things'. This, the adventure of flavour, is his motivation. His goal is rather more spiritual: to express, through his cooking, the meaning of civilisation, to capture the essence of culture—just as, for Lawrence Durrell, the spirit of the Mediterranean was epitomised by its black olives:

> *The whole Mediterranean, the sculpture, the palms, the gold beads, the bearded heroes, the wine, the ideas, the ships, the moonlight, the winged gorgons, the bronze men, the philosophers—all of it seems to rise in the sour, pungent taste of these black olives between the teeth.*

Silk purses from sows' ears? Is it not an odd ambition, to take so substantial and so transient a material as food, and transform it in such a way that it represents a notion as abstract and enduring as civilisation or culture? If it were bronze, in the hands of Rodin, or words from the pen of Balzac, or music from the genius of Beethoven...surely these idealistic concepts are better expressed through other media?

Cheong appears ignorant of any hint of paradox. Breaking with traditional associations does not daunt him; he is a free spirit, a Puck who takes inspiration from wherever the senses invite him. In his Kuala Lumpur childhood, Cheong remembers himself as an observer, living above the family shop near the Ampang bus terminal, fascinated by the food, smells and people of this crossroads of cultures. He describes himself now as a 'passer by' who finds a scent he likes, a colour that appeals, and from these impressions creates his own masterpiece.

To describe him as a proponent of 'East meets West' is simplistic; Cheong is truly multicultural in his approach to food, and freely admits that he is not satisfied with the cuisine of merely one culture. Take his Lamb Sahara—it begins with lamb marinated in soy sauce and ginger juice, which is then cooked with carrots, onions, chillis and peppers, flavoured with tahini and lemon juice...

Some people will have reservations about what seems to be haphazard appropriation. Certainly, I feel a vague disquiet at the idea of 'taking', at will—though I also know that evolution is natural, and that to place constraints around a cuisine, or any other form of cultural expression, is to render it artificial and, ultimately, sterile.

But Cheong's borrowings are made with discrimination and sensitivity. Modestly, he acknowledges that he is not a trained chef, and therefore obliged to rely more on his senses, and on an 'inbuilt' food sense and sensibility. He grew up in a household in which food was important, surrounded by different cultures. His family was Cantonese, one of the few Cantonese households in a mainly Hokkien street; in the street behind were Indians, and on the other side of the bus station, by the riverside, were the stalls of the Malays. Most Chinese families were conservative in their tastes, remaining within their particular province, but Cheong's family was exceptionally adventurous, sampling the dishes of different cultures. And they talked food: which particular restaurant to go to, for which particular dish; where to buy the best ingredients.

The scents of spices (which still, he says, send him to heaven), of onions and chillies drying on nets, illustrate his memories of this milieu, but the most significant influence on Cheong's developing passion was his grandmother. Matriarch of the household, she would daily prepare—with the help of her daughters—lunch and dinner for 30 or so, in three sittings. In the process, she would explain to the daughters—and anyone else who happened to be listening—how a particular dish was to taste, how to achieve the right texture, which techniques to apply, at the same time as demonstrating this flavour, this texture, these techniques. More importantly, she taught them the three fundamentals of the Cantonese repertoire: steamed white chicken, steamed whole fish, stir-fried vegetables.

Cheong was 'fated'—so he says—to be a chef and restaurateur. His great-grandfather had a restaurant in the tin-and-rubber Malaysian hinterland. His grandfather, after moving to the capital to ensure a better education for the next generation, also ran restaurants, as well as the general store near the bus station, which ensured a steady supply of spices and other ingredients to the restaurant in the country. His father, a poultry farmer, opened a restaurant—partly to advertise his produce, partly to use it: an instinctive example of vertical integration. Cheong helped out in this restaurant, cooking meals for the staff—who would call out advice and instructions between comings and goings. It was all part of a learning process which encouraged sensory discrimination, emphasised individual judgment and assumed a certain responsiveness of the reflexes.

But the fate of youth is to rebel, to refuse fate. Cheong began to study electronics—which is what brought him to Australia. Wanting extra money, he started working in a hotel, making sandwiches—except on Fridays when, in addition, he would help the pub cook make her Friday specials: steak sandwiches, chop suey, curried sausages... Next was a brief stint in a Chinese restaurant in Melbourne where he started to learn about mass catering—vast batches of fried rice every night. Back in Adelaide, he was soon cooking Greek food at the Illiad—and learning about it, both from the black-draped elders rolling vine leaves into dolmades and from Elizabeth David's first book, *Mediterranean Food.*

Next move was to a curry restaurant, Kitcheners, which shared its kitchen with that of the adjoining steakhouse, Moos. When the chef of that part of the house left, Cheong was allowed to take over—and not long after, the standard carrots-and-broccoli-with-cheese-sauce accompaniment to the standard steak diane-beef stroganoff became a lightly spiced vegetable stir-fry. People liked it. This, he says, marked the beginning of a change in the Australian palate. It happened in 1974, the same year that Bocuse and Guérard visited and scattered the seeds of nouvelle cuisine.

After such a variety of culinary experiences it was natural that, when asked to prepare a buffet selection for a wine bar, Cheong should propose a model based on his home territory around the Ampang bus terminal: cultural diversity, as represented by rare roast beef and horseradish sauce, American spareribs, Indian curries, some Asian dishes and a Malaysian colonial salad of tuna, cucumbers and chilli. And this was the formula which launched Neddy's, towards the end of 1975—the restaurant Adelaide had been waiting for.

Cheong calls Neddy's a 'natural Australian restaurant' which, from its very beginning, was multicultural—a combination of Greek, Indian, Chinese, Malay and other dishes. In the mix-and-match, unisex, peace-prompting '70s, it seemed perfectly natural, to Cheong at least, to juxtapose different cultures, to ignore proprietary rights. Here, at Neddy's, his culinary adventure really started; he read more and more about food, about the traditions, lifestyles and beliefs of particular regions, and developed his conviction that the fundamental qualities of any dish were texture and flavour, and appropriateness to lifestyle.

In Cheong's opinion, it is more important to achieve this than to strive for authenticity; more important that today's ingredients can be brought together in harmony, that the flavours marry, join together and become one. This has remained his philosophy: I do it my way. But underlying 'Cheong's way' are what he calls his Chinese instincts. As Asian vegetables, herbs and spices were incorporated into what was, at base, a European cuisine, Neddy's menu began to display a greater uniformity, and individualistic style. For over ten years Neddy's showed the way for other restaurants, and Cheong became progressively more fascinated by Chinese traditions. (The best Chinese restaurant in town was undoubtedly Neddy's on Monday nights, with its superb five-course, whim-of-the-chef dinner; I remember the crispness of his fried chicken, the meltingly soft texture of slow-cooked lamb, the velvety richness of the final bowl of broth.)

News of Cheong's return, after seven years' teaching at the Regency Hotel School, caused more that a flutter of excitement in Adelaide—not mere parochialism, for this is an event of national significance. His original style —not so much an East-West fusion as Asian cuisine clad in French *couture*— has been influential in forming a generation of new chefs all over Australia and has made a distinct impression on Adelaide (which, he believes, provides his best audience of adventurous and appreciative eaters).

Cheong's cuisine is typically complex, in a way that even the best prawn *bisque,* the most perfectly executed *sauce bercy*, is not...

Cheong's complexity is discreet; no qualifications are needed to appreciate his food, since his talent lies in combining flavours and textures into a single but multidimensional taste experience which goes beyond the palate to the intellect... For me, Cheong is a culinary magician, a sorcerer of the kitchen.

His Asian background has given him a familiarity with spices which European-born colleagues often lack, and from which derives his talent at marrying flavours—rice perfumed with black cardamom, cinnamon, saffron and others, served at a 'Bedouin' banquet. I doubt that Cheong could cook without spices which, for him, convey certain symbolic qualities; in particular, they are associated with death. For Cheong believes that food must contain an element of mystique; in the soul of the dish is the meaning of existence. The dish becomes, in a way, sacramental. To achieve this is, for Cheong, the challenge, so that in the eating the mystery may be assimilated. Perhaps not everyone will be able to understand and appreciate it—as not everyone responds to Rodin's *Le Penseur*—but it should be there, for the initiates, and for those who take the trouble to pursue 'the flavour of things'.

This foreword was originally published as an article in The Sydney Review, *June 1993*

Cheong

I am the third child in my family. In Kuala Lumpur, in Malaysia, the extended Liew family consisted of about 200, all of whom used to gather regularly for the major annual events such as Chinese New Year, All Soul's Day and grandmother's birthday.

We lived on High Street, now known as Jalan Bandar, very close to the Ampang Station, a travel depot where people caught buses to other states in Malaysia. It was a natural site for a market where travellers could buy clothing, trinkets and food. My favourite stall was that of the Indian kachang man. He sold kachang puteh, roasted white beans; muruku, like an Indian version of a pretzel made from chickpea flour; vadai, which resembles felafel; and a variety of fried beans and lentils. Just across the road were numerous restaurants—Malay, Indian, Chinese—including the Chinese barbecue stalls with the most basic of tables and chairs, selling the equivalent of fast food.

Our street was typically Chinese, mostly inhabited by Hokkien tea traders. We were among the very few Cantonese families. Next to us was a Chinese herbalist, with every possible variety of fresh herb; the most pungent and overpowering smell was of rutha—a plant that is supposed to remove poison from the body. Then there was a Teh Chew restaurant serving mainly rice congee, considered a very healthy and restorative dish. Sometimes the congee was served with sweet potato, a reminder of the Japanese occupation when people had no rice and lived entirely on sweet potato. The restaurant had a master stock full of duck and chicken, offal, pork ears and intestines, bean curd and pickles to go with the congee.

There was also a Hokkien restaurant renowned for its noodles. I especially liked their fried prawn and pumpkin patty, the same size and shape as a frisbee; we kids could buy one for about 15 cents, and they were our preferred fast food. On the same street there was a Chinese coffee shop and another herbalist specialising in dried rather than fresh herbs and prepared medicines.

Different hawkers came and went all day, walking with baskets, pushing their barrows or riding tricycles, depending on their wares. At around eight the breakfast sellers would arrive. One of the first temptations was rice vermicelli cake with palm sugar. Then a Chinese lady would come with her nonya sweets, and around ten, the laksa man, always to the same familiar spot. At noon the yong tow fu man would come on his tricycle, bearing the vegetables and beancurd stuffed with fish farce.

At three or four in the afternoon the rojak seller would enter the scene and at five, the soup man with red bean soup, peanut soup, black rice soup and black sesame soup, all eaten with coconut milk. These sweet soups were regarded as rejuvenating tonics. (There are restaurants entirely devoted to preparing and serving this type of soup and inhabited especially by women seeking perpetually youthful looks. You will find such places in Sydney today.)

Our shop house was near a junction of three roads. We were the local poultry wholesalers selling live chicks, chickens and chicken feed. We lived upstairs—as is the way in shop houses even today. At that time life was fairly traditional for our family. The women of the household wore cheong sam or the traditional shirt and loose trousers; they were not allowed to perm their hair or wear Western-style slacks or high heels by order of my grandmother who wielded matriarchal power in the household. She controlled the kitchen and the ways of the house. My mother was allowed to help but not to cook. Most of our food was from my grandmother's province. She did not cook Malay or nonya dishes.

My memories of that time are mainly of my grandmother's birthday and her funeral, my cousin's wedding and the many hours when I sat with my aunties in the kitchen preparing sour dough buns, cleaning shark fin, removing the young shoots from the lotus seeds, cutting the wood, stoking the kitchen fire and cleaning the vegetables. Other strong memories are of making chilli sauce, and grinding rice to make flour, using two flat granite stones the size of car tyres as a rotating mill. In retrospect, this was all part of my apprenticeship.

Festivals were special food preparation experiences. The Jung Festival was the time to make packets of glutinous rice filled with meat or beans, or a Malaysian-style shrimp and chilli combination, then to wrap them in bamboo leaves to form a pyramid. During Chinese New Year I would watch grandma make red-cooked pork with taro root, which required steaming for many hours. I can also remember picking the feathers out of bird nests to prepare for a birthday breakfast.

My father decided to move to the farm, 8 kilometres away, when I was about fourteen, after my grandmother died. The shop became our Cantonese restaurant where I worked during school vacations. Every year we brought in live fish for Chinese New Year and we would do our spit roast at the back of the shop—up to six pigs roasted at a time and turned by hand. At the back we also used a large wok to fry rock salt, used for baking chicken, and our rice was steamed in giant wooden tubs. Our wok cookers were fuelled with gas in cylinders—a change from the old wood fuelled method.

The farm was about 4.5 hectares in size, spreading over two hill faces, with terraces on three levels. Five families lived together there. Bananas of every variety and tapioca plantings stopped soil erosion, tea-tree bushes were abundant, and there were many fruit trees, including star fruit, mango, rambutan, and mangosteen. We had vegetable gardens planted with such things as sweet potato and sugar cane; fish ponds; and there were the inevitable rows of chicken sheds. Water was drawn from a well and we generated our own electricity. There were dogs—lots of them—to guard the farm.

Our place was situated near a Malay kampong, or village, a stream acting as a natural boundary between our farm and the kampong. During Hari Raya, the Malay New Year, we were offered many Malay dishes and we were often invited to come to the colourful village weddings. There was no danger of ever going hungry on the farm—food was all around us, a paradise for those old expatriates who had suffered near starvation in China. I remember digging up tapioca roots. My sister Kwei-lan would make this into pudding and whatever was left we would sell to the villagers for pocket money. We were expert at killing, dressing and roasting chickens on an open fire, and we collected eggs for cooking omelettes or 'purse' eggs. Much understanding can be gained from cooking eggs—you need technique and patience to be successful. If we were thirsty then we could drink fresh sugar-cane juice.

This was the time when I started to cook for others. I would fry sweet potato leaves as a vegetable dish with dried shrimp and chilli, cook omelettes with baked beans—an early experience of being creative with tins—and deep-fry chicken as my mother had taught me. Pan frying our fish in butter showed European influence. Chicken and potato stew was another regular dish which we all learnt to prepare. For dessert, there were coconut sweets.

After Grandma died we had to make our own sweets for Chinese New Year. For the first time my mother was in charge of making the celebration tapioca pudding and rice-flour biscuits, rather than being a mere helper. In this period new cultural influences emerged in our cuisine, changing what had been a very traditional Chinese table. It was a time for loosening traditions and absorbing other influences and becoming a 'modern Chinese family' in our own eyes, a transitional time. Before my grandmother's death we had not cooked many curry dishes; after her death this changed. We started introducing other styles partly because we liked the flavours and partly because we simply did not have the knowledge and the time for traditional cookery which my grandmother had possessed. Working in a restaurant meant less time for my parents, so convenience was an important factor, hence the arrival of tinned baked beans on our shelves. Cold stores selling butter, milk, ham and other Western goods suddenly appeared. I especially remember chocolates and walnuts becoming available and tinned sausages. Daughters in the family were learning home economics at school. They made cakes and biscuits while Elvis and the Beatles played on the radio, and brought home new methods—whipping eggs for a sponge was labour intensive, so we all pitched in.

The other chief influence upon our cookery was our interest in and exposure to Malay tastes. On the farm we had to walk more than a kilometre to find tasty Malay food, so the alternative was to try preparing it ourselves. Also, living on the edge of a kampong brought us out of our very Chinese milieu in the town and brought us into close contact with Malay culture and its village food traditions. Meanwhile the modern poultry journals taught us how to do barbecue or Kentucky fried style chicken—another source of change.

In five families there was an endless procession of birthdays, allowing me plenty of experience of the preparations—salt-baked chicken, plum meat, tungpo pork, trotters in vinegar, and a range of dried foods like shark's fin were typical birthday foods. My father's older brother often cooked and knew a great deal about traditional Chinese cookery, and his younger brother was always regarded as a gourmet (his wife used Chinese cookbooks to expand her repertoire). These were my teachers and some of my earliest influences.

This book is about my continuing culinary journey, after I came to Australia at the age of 20, and discovered new influences to add to the old.

Liz

'You know, Liz, you should always cut up your chicken bones finely when you are making stock—that's what I tell my students every Monday—otherwise you don't get all the flavour out of your chicken...oh, and don't even *think* about throwing in the celery stalk ends before the stock has boiled. It will discolour. Put them in with the diced vegetables after boiling...'

The moral of this story is do not expect to escape without some invaluable advice if you decide to cook in front of Cheong. I've been making stock passably well for years—but always in a hurry and with my mother's wartime advice ('waste not want not') ringing in my ears—now there is something else to learn. This is Cheong's gift or mania for the essentials, an instinct for the ultimate combination, a quest for perfection married with the desire to surprise. 'Anything is possible', was Neddy's slogan; it's still Cheong's signature statement.

Cheong and I are an unlikely culinary partnership—I lead too hectic a life to cook as often or as carefully as I would like, but I enjoy exploring different cuisines and discovering what makes a dish great, what makes it mediocre and what makes it fail. While I was fortunate to have a mother who rarely used anything tinned or ready-made, and whose English home cooking was always enjoyable, I can chiefly thank a New Caledonian mixed-race family—Chinese, English, French and Melanesian—for awakening my appreciation of fine cuisine. I thank my adventurous parents for making French forever music to my ears, regular visits to New Caledonia were the first of my multicultural journeys. Madame Frouin was up at dawn every day to make the cafe au lait, served in Chinese bowls and eaten with a baguette or brioche. This was for the extended family, and while she started in the kitchen, her French husband, the local baker, shopkeeper and raconteur with the clown's face, tended the bread. Two hours before dejeuner at 11, they would have begun their preparations: a fine soup, freshly caught pan-fried fish, a 'heart of cocotier' salad (if a cyclone had kindly felled a coconut palm), a gratin of vegetables, perhaps fresh cockles enveloped in a cream sauce and served with rice, vin rouge—watered down for the children, full strength for the adults—and plenty of Frouin bread were typical everyday luncheon dishes. After the evening meal, the family often enjoyed the classic French dessert, Oeufs a la Neige, and there was always wonderful fruit, especially the soursop or English durian as the Malaysians call it. The lapping of the waves was just audible during our mealtimes, occasionally drowned out by Mr Frouin exclaiming, as he ate his favourite tiny pickled green chillies, 'Ca pique! Ca pique!'

Not only was I exposed to excellent home cuisine, I came close to the realities, like the day the pig was slaughtered. As soon as its black bristles had been scraped off in steaming water, the whole family worked to use up nearly every piece of it—pâtés, potted meat, sausages made with the intestines, and so on throughout the day. This was when the true meaning of delicatessen was revealed to an Adelaide teenager of the mid-sixties, fresh from the great Australian ugliness.

Marrying a man with a Malaysian-Chinese background introduced me to another great world cuisine—an experience for which I am endlessly grateful. John's mother, Thin Lian Siew, and amah, Foon Chay, both shared cooking secrets with me, some of which are buried in this book; there were ingredients, tastes, smells and textures which were revelations to me and which I have always tried without hesitation. Despite all their predictions that the kwei-lo (white devil woman) would never take to the rotten fragrance of the durian I ate it triumphantly. In Malaysia, material life was precarious for many, which helped me to understand the Chinese preoccupation with food. Food is precious, and this might be your last day on earth, so what is there to be eaten *must* be cooked well or one might as well not eat it at all.

We started to become friendly with Cheong and Mary when their second child, Alice, was a small baby and our first, Francesca, was *in utero*. I remember inviting them both to lunch and serving a fresh tomato soup which they both admired. I recall feeling relieved and secretly wondering whether they were being polite. It's not easy to cook for two people who live and breathe food and who are running the most adventurous restaurant in Adelaide. It was a favourite place for John and me and our friends, and our first child, Francesca. Summer in the courtyard and exquisite warm salads; cold nights and rich venison or kangaroo; Chinese banquets on Mondays when John would relish a childhood favourite, pork hock. I often think how fortunate we were to experience such talent in a rather provincial city.

What apart from a love of good food led me to co-author this book? I would have to say the lure of writing and of exploring new notions of Australian culture. To quote David Malouf, in *The Australian*:

> *Is, for example, the emergence of what we call Modern Australian cuisine—the crossing of old Australian with Mediterranean and Asian elements to make an entirely new form of cooking—the expression in another form of the language we speak, boldly appropriating and adapting, pushing the rules, to arrive, by an eclectic and improvisory process, at a mixture that works?*

This book flows easily from many stimulating discussions at Cheong and Mary's table, with our children sometimes listening. Andre, Alice, Eugenia, and Stephanie Liew and Francesca and Sebastian Ho have absorbed the 'taste' knowledge of everything from good cheeses to slippery Chinese beef tendon at that table. Writing this book is also the natural culmination of many marvellous dinners at Neddy's and at Adelaide Festival literary banquets in which Cheong and I collaborated. It especially embodies both of our families' daily living and thinking, where cultural inheritances mix and mingle, creating something new.

Neddy's Classic

Helen Barraclough and Joe McEvoy had a little city restaurant called Neddy's Kitchen in Hutt Street, Adelaide. It had old photos of chemist shops and other memorabilia hanging on the wall—and they served country-style food, wholesome and unpretentious. Their old dog, Yellow, roamed around the restaurant.

It was called Neddy's Kitchen because Helen's nickname was Ned (she had a great interest in horses, and Joe had been a rodeo star). Diners were drawn by the hearty traditional home cooking and the bargain-basement prices. We were all disappointed when we heard it was changing hands and wondered what would be on offer. Little did we know that Adelaide cuisine was about to be launched…enter Cheong…

I started Neddy's with my wife Mary Ziukelis and friends Barry and Rennie Ross. We had all worked together at a curry restaurant called Lord Kitchener's, and we went into the restaurant armed only with the understanding that I could cook and Barry could run the front of house while Rennie and Mary could mastermind the desserts and be our mainstays. At first we had no fixed approach: I simply designed a menu around what was available at the morning market.

Our blackboard menu ended up providing the direction that we lacked at the outset. It evolved into a more regular but always multicultural menu as I drew on experiences from my life and work in Greek, Indian,

South-East Asian, French and Chinese kitchens. Meanwhile the front of house had attracted the personalities and local colour that made Neddy's unique—the place to be seen if you were, or thought you were, in the avant garde.

It was a meeting place for lawyers, journalists, politicians, the business brigade—doing deals over lunch in the days when lunch was tax deductible.

The night time trade was different—quiet, serious diners after a new eating experience. Barry's flair for colour was expressed in the green and pink decor—very unusual for a seventies restaurant, but it worked well. Artist Jo Caddy made us a glazed terracotta merman for the courtyard, which was transformed into a leafy retreat with kentia palms, herbs, and hydrangeas. Each day we decorated the dining room with fresh-cut flowers, in a very natural style. Informality, a welcoming setting and serious food became the distinctive qualities of Neddy's.

In the kitchen, the menu was based on fresh produce combined in simple dishes—from steak to nonya curry, or Chinese beef spare ribs to a Greek lobster a la Plaka. Mary and Rennie designed the dessert menu, including chocolate figs, English trifle with fresh berries, and rigo jansci—a Hungarian chocolate dessert.

We pored over cookbooks for new ideas and delectable and interesting dishes to add to our repertoire. Janet Jeffs, our first apprentice, brought professional skills into the kitchen, and our menus became more formal under her influence. I learnt from the apprentice and she learnt from me—not at all the usual way in the Chinese or French tradition, where the master chef is the fount of all knowledge.

We introduced game dishes to our menu and to Adelaide, including kangaroo, venison, turkey, goose, pheasant, guinea fowl and quail.

In 1981 Barry left to open Possums, leading to the now famous partnership with Philip Searle, and eventually the Oasis Seros in Sydney.

I was determined to create a new dimension in eating for Adelaide, based on multicultural dishes but with formal qualities. I also wanted to express my Chinese heritage more fully, so Monday nights became banquet nights. We offered diners a style of Chinese banquet rarely or never experienced by people of European origin in Australia. Gutsier-style northern dishes reflected the inspiration of a recent trip to northern China, and the closest European equivalent was the big-flavoured Mediterranean style. I always thought northern Chinese flavours would appeal to Australians—the thin grilled slices of beef Mongolian style, buns rather than rice, the big cuts of meat, and the pickled and preserved vegetables like those from European countries with very cold winters. The banquets were also an experiment to see whether these dishes would be accepted, and the techniques appreciated.

I also introduced some of the Chinese festival traditions to Neddy's. We held Moon Festival and Chinese New Year banquets where we changed the setting of the dining room to suit the mood of the occasion and create a tone of Chinese hospitality. These were jovial celebrations, full of bonhomie, lots of food and drink and friendship, just as the Chinese would expect them to be. Regular customers wrote poetic descriptions of the dishes, and Tim John, this book's illustrator, did the graphics, so there was a sense of shared fun.

The banquet dishes influenced my weekly menu and some eventually became part of the regular menu. Barry Ross and Philip Searle would often turn up on Mondays and we would discuss style and techniques until the early hours. We agreed that the food should have our own personal stamp—in other words, our dishes should not conform to standard classical notions. If we had an unspoken motto it was prob-ably 'Break the Rules'. My own saying, which eventually found its way into Tim John's graphics, was 'Anything is Possible'.

And anything *was* possible. One of the famous stories of this period was the deer penis saga. I was asked to prepare a special dinner for winemakers in 1985 and it just so happened that fresh deer penis was available at the time. Deer penis is regarded as an aphrodisiac in some cultures, but I did not announce it on the menu. We cut it into diamond shapes and served it in a game soup—the last dish on the menu in traditional Chinese style. The winemakers raved about it and the fateful question had to be answered. Somehow the word got out and Neddy's was instantly notorious. I am not sure it did us a lot of good, but the winemakers went on to make some very robust wine in 1986!

During this time Julie Ziukelis was an apprentice, as were Tim Pak Poy and Lorraine Nelson. We would often talk about our appreciation of food—you must be able to appreciate good food before you can ever cook well. When Tim wanted to learn my style and all the techniques I was using, I said that I could only offer guidance. This was the message for all my apprentices—just reproducing technique cannot replace personal talent and the determination to pursue the art. Tim regarded this as the most important advice I ever gave him.

Leading chefs like Urs Inauen will argue that Australia needs to avoid catering for fashion and concentrate on building a solid culinary tradition like those in Europe and Asia. There one finds a strong food culture where many restaurants offer the same familiar regional dishes each season. But our country's geography and climate mean that 'seasons' are not so relevant. If it is not in season in the south then it will be abundant in the north, so the smorgasbord of possibilities for the chef is endless. In Australia the blurring of seasonal difference, the lack of a solid food culture and the influence of multiculturalism result in a constantly evolving style.

This was certainly true at Neddy's, especially in the latter period when I pushed back the barriers, both in the style of service and presentation, and in the dishes themselves. The content of the dish might be more European, but it could be served simultaneously with others, like a Chinese table, or sequentially, like a Chinese banquet. The informality of this approach suits easy-going friendship—mateship, really—which is very Australian.

Neddy's Classic recipes

WARM SALAD OF MORETON BAY BUGS
WITH TOASTED SALTED FISH

STEAMED CUCUMBER AND LAMBS' BRAINS
WITH SPICY TOMATO SAUCE

TEA-SMOKED QUAIL, PRESERVED EGGS AND GLACÉ GINGER
IN SWEET PASTRY

TIMBALE OF JELLIED PRAWNS AND STEAMED PHEASANT
WITH MUSTARD GREEN SALAD

SPICY CALAMARI WITH SWAMP CABBAGE
AND CHILLI HOI SIN SAUCE

SHARK LIPS, SCALLOPS AND SEA CUCUMBER
BRAISED IN CARROT OIL

KANGAROO FILLET, VEAL TONGUE
AND BRAISED WITLOF

ROAST SUCKLING PIG WITH GREEN GINGER WINE
AND SPICED SPINACH PURÉE

ANISE AND GINGER FLAVOURED DUCK
WITH STEAMED LOTUS BUN

RHUBARB TART WITH CLOVE CREAM
AND CHOCOLATE FIGS

BLACK RICE AND PALM SUGAR
PUDDING

Warm salad of Moreton Bay bugs with toasted salted fish

This dish was inspired by a visit to Singapore where my parents tried a simple bean sprout dish with toasted Asian salted fish, rather like the well-known Mediterranean bacalhau or salted cod. (Incidentally, salted fish was introduced to Asia by the colonial Portuguese traders.) In the late 1970s Moreton Bay bugs had just hit the commercial seafood market and they were very much in demand. I decided to accompany them with snow peas and to add the simple Chinese combination of salted fish and bean sprouts. I finished it with a vinaigrette. It is the vinaigrette, combined with the flavour of the toasted fish, that makes the dish so appetising. This dish was on our menu for some time and we had quite a few complaints when we finally took it off. The decision to call it a warm salad was inspired by contemporary European menus—it could have been described as a warm stir-fry but with a little composition thrown in!

Prepare the ingredients for this dish in advance, ready to be cooked immediately before serving. A sensible order is to make the purée first, the salted fish second, followed by the snow peas. The Moreton Bay bugs and bean sprouts are the final elements of the dish.

Avocado purée

1 ripe avocado
juice of ½ lemon
1 tablespoon virgin olive oil

salt
freshly ground black pepper

Warm salad

200 g snow peas
18 Moreton Bay bugs
salt

freshly ground black pepper
1 tablespoon virgin olive oil

Salted fish

20 g Asian salted fish
1 tablespoon peanut oil
salt
1 dried chilli
1 clove garlic, crushed
1 slice ginger

100 g bean sprouts
2 spring onions, chopped
24 frisée lettuce leaves, pale
24 rocket leaves
24 lamb's lettuce leaves

Vinaigrette

2 tablespoons peanut oil
2 tablespoons grapeseed oil
4 tablespoons champagne vinegar
juice of 1 lime

juice of ½ orange
2 teaspoons Dijon mustard
salt
freshly ground black pepper

Avocado purée

Mash the avocado with a fork. Add the lemon juice and the virgin olive oil and season with salt and pepper. Mix together or blend to a smooth purée. Leave the stone in the purée to prevent discolouration, cover with plastic wrap and set aside.

Warm salad

Blanch the snow peas in salted water and set aside. Using scissors, cut along the sides of the belly of the bugs, lift meat from shells and season with salt and pepper. Heat the olive oil in a frying-pan and sauté the bugs a few at a time for about half a minute each side. Remove and keep warm.

Salted fish

Slice the salted fish thinly. In a wok or frying-pan, heat the peanut oil and sprinkle with salt. Add chilli, garlic, slice of ginger and salted fish and fry until crisp. Remove the salted fish and reserve other ingredients for garnish. In the wok, toss the bean sprouts and spring onions, followed by frisée lettuce, rocket and lamb's lettuce, and stir quickly and rhythmically to warm through only, not to cook.

Vinaigrette

Combine all ingredients thoroughly.

Composition

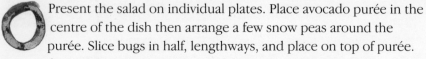 Present the salad on individual plates. Place avocado purée in the centre of the dish then arrange a few snow peas around the purée. Slice bugs in half, lengthways, and place on top of purée. Arrange bean sprout mixture on top of the bugs and drizzle with vinaigrette. Garnish with the crispy salted fish.

Steamed cucumber and lambs' brains with spicy tomato sauce

In the late 1970s, several Adelaide restaurants were featuring lambs' brains with white or red beurre blanc on their entrée menus. Inspired by my grandmother, who used to serve steamed pigs' brains as a soup with a custard base, I developed this dish, which was among the first of my own style of recipes. I remember serving it to veteran Australian gourmet, Len Evans, who promptly recommended it to his friends and took down the recipe.

A timeless, satisfying dish and classic Neddy's. Despite its Chinese inspiration, the shape and size of the finished 'crèmes', and the use of the lamb, speak of France. Culturally, the dish translates well—a soft savoury egg custard enjoyed by both the East and West. Cucumber enhances the gingery lambs' brains and the rich sauce, which in turn adds colour and a hint of sharpness. The marinade for the brains replaces the traditional acidulated aromatic stock used in the French preparation. Fresh brains are essential to the success of this dish.

Cucumber and lambs' brains

6 sets very fresh lambs' brains
1 litre ice-cold water
1 slice lemon
1 teaspoon salt
1 teaspoon finely chopped ginger
1 teaspoon finely chopped spring
   onion, white only
1 tablespoon yellow rice wine,
   Shaoshing variety

½ teaspoon sesame oil
1 tablespoon oyster sauce
peanut oil to grease moulds
1 cucumber, thinly sliced
   lengthways and seeded
3 eggs
300 ml milk
salt
freshly ground black pepper

Spicy tomato sauce

2½ tablespoons fresh tomato
   purée (see page 221)
1 tablespoon oyster sauce

3 drops Tabasco sauce
1 tablespoon white wine
1 tablespoon sugar

Garnish

½ spring onion extra, white only,
   finely shredded into 'angel hair'

fresh coriander

Cucumber and lambs' brains

Put brains in the ice-cold water and soak for 30 minutes. Starting from the underside of the brains, carefully remove the arteries under cold running water. If the brains are very fresh this should not be difficult. Add the slice of lemon and salt to some clean water and bring to the boil. Plunge brains in the boiling water, remove the pot from the flame and allow the brains to steep for about 3 minutes. Remove the brains from the pan and dry with kitchen paper. Combine the ginger, spring onion, rice wine, sesame oil and oyster sauce in a bowl. Cut the brains in quarters and marinate them in the mixture for 10 minutes.

Lightly oil six dariole moulds, or full-size coffee cups, with peanut oil. Working from the centre, arrange the thin slices of cucumber on the base and sides of the mould, slightly overlapping each slice. Place four pieces of brains in each mould.

To make a custard, mix eggs with milk, season with salt and pepper and pour into moulds to cover the contents, then fold over the cucumber. Cover each mould with plastic wrap and gently steam for 20 to 25 minutes in a bain-marie or Chinese bamboo steamer.

Spicy tomato sauce

Prepare the sauce while the custard is steaming. In a pan, mix together tomato purée, oyster sauce, Tabasco, wine and sugar and stir until the mixture is shiny and coats the back of a spoon.

Composition

Turn the custard out onto kitchen paper to absorb excess liquid. Using a spatula, carefully transfer the custard from the paper to the plate and pour sauce around each mould. Garnish with coriander leaves and shredded spring onion.

Tea-smoked quail, preserved eggs and glacé ginger in sweet pastry

In the 1980s we were playing around a lot with Sichuan tea-smoked duck and decided to do a variation with quail, combining both Chinese green-tea leaves and Australian gum leaves. The Chinese would have used pork or chicken rather than quail. I decided to capture the salt and sweet combinations so loved by the Chinese in a rich pastry with preserved duck eggs. The eggs are preserved by wrapping them in a mixture of lime and ash, then burying them in the ground for approximately 100 days. A rich black jelly forms under the shell and the yolk develops five rings, graduating from black to grey. This is definitely an experience of 'black is beautiful' and also expensive! The taste is distinctive and slightly sharp, stimulating the salivary glands. We found that with a garnish of bitter green salad it made a great entrée dish. The typical Australian reaction at the time was tentative—the eggs were the reason for this—but with encouragement most guests would try it and discover its delights. The quail available then were the large Japanese variety.

This dish demands patience and precision. Begin by marinating and cooking the quail, then follow with the filling, and finally the pastry crust. The combination of meat filling, quail, ginger and preserved eggs is layered onto a rich pastry base and then covered with another round of pastry, each one made separately for individual plates. A simple side salad with walnut-oil dressing and quail legs is served with this rich, savoury, sweet-crust dish.

Marinade

1 teaspoon honey
   (preferably lucerne)
½ tablespoon lime juice

2 tablespoons peanut oil
salt
freshly ground black pepper

Smoked quail

6 whole quail
salt
freshly ground black pepper
½ packet lychee tea leaves

handful gum leaves
3 sprigs thyme
3 sprigs sage

Filling

1 teaspoon cornflour
1 tablespoon light soy sauce
½ teaspoon sesame oil
150 g pork fillet, thinly sliced
3 chicken livers
1 tablespoon butter
1 tablespoon peanut oil

1 teaspoon finely chopped garlic
1 teaspoon finely chopped ginger
6 abalone mushrooms, sliced
2 spring onions, cut into
   4 cm lengths
2 tablespoons medium sherry

Pastry crust

900 g sweet-crust pastry
   (see page 231)
2 preserved black eggs (known
   as 1000-year-old eggs)

6 pieces glacé ginger, sliced
clarified butter
1 egg, lightly beaten

Dressing

½ tablespoon walnut oil
juice of ½ lemon

1 tablespoon white wine, chardonnay
freshly ground black pepper

Salad

½ bunch watercress
½ frisée lettuce, pale leaves only

Marinade

To make the marinade, warm the honey and then mix in the lime juice and peanut oil. Season to taste.

Smoked quail

Season the quail with salt and pepper and then brush them with the honey marinade. Moisten the tea leaves, gum leaves, thyme and sage with a little water. Using a wok with a lid and a steaming rack (or a large steamer), put aluminium foil in the base and sprinkle with the leaves and herbs. Put wok over a flame and heat until the leaves smoke. Put quail on steaming rack, place over smoke, and cover with a lid. Smoke for

4 minutes over medium heat. Turn off the heat and leave quail in the 'smoker' for a further 6 minutes. Remove quail breasts and legs, setting aside the legs for the salad, and discard the bones.

Filling

Mix together the cornflour, soy and sesame oil. Marinate the sliced pork fillet in this mixture for 15 minutes.

Sauté the chicken livers for a few minutes in the butter and then cut livers into quarters.

In a frying-pan heat the peanut oil and sauté the garlic and ginger. Add the pork fillet, mushrooms, spring onion and chopped liver and flame with the sherry. Chill the mixture in the fridge.

Pastry crust

Preheat the oven to 190°C. Roll out the pastry to a thickness of 3 mm. Using a 10 cm pastry cutter, cut out 6 circles and place on a baking sheet. Arrange fillet mixture in the centre of each circle, leaving a border of pastry measuring about 5 mm.

Slice each egg into thirds. Place a piece of egg and a piece of glacé ginger on top of each mound of filling mixture and then two quail breasts. Cut 6 more pastry circles and lightly brush the beaten egg over the bottom edge of each circle. Lay each circle over the quail, gently pressing down the glazed border. Brush the top of the pastry with egg wash and chill for 20 minutes, then bake in the preheated oven for 10 minutes. Remove from the oven and brush the tops with clarified butter.

Dressing

Make a dressing with the walnut oil, lemon juice, wine and pepper.

Composition

 Arrange a salad of watercress, frisée lettuce and quail legs to the side of each plate and drizzle over the dressing. Place a pastry circle in the centre of each plate.

Timbale of jellied prawns and steamed pheasant with mustard green salad

Perfectly cooked southern king prawns make this dish one of my favourite summer appetisers. It suits the climate and atmosphere of summer. To me, it is more an Asian-style European dish. Some of its special features include blanching of the mustard green stems until they are very soft and tender, then chilling them. The choice of English mustard reflects the Chinese taste for sharpness: it brings out the flavour, and the mustard opens up the sauce. Whenever there is a Chinese wedding this is the favourite entrée dish. I remember it was always served in my dad's restaurant outside Kuala Lumpur.

Is this dish European or Chinese? Who gave it to whom? It has a foot in both the West and the East.

South Australian prawns are among the best in the world. The season for southern king prawns is very short—about four months—and if you cannot obtain them, substitute tiger prawns. You could substitute chicken for pheasant, making a less rich but still effective dish.

The preparation of this dish requires time and concentration. The chicken fumet should be prepared one day in advance. The clarification, which must be carefully executed, produces a crystal-clear consommé which is the essence of this dish.

Timbales

chicken consommé (see page 225)
2 medium-sized ripe tomatoes
12 quail eggs
24 small abalone mushrooms
⅔ tablespoon olive oil
salt

freshly ground black pepper
75 g pickled ginger, Japanese
24 medium-sized prawns,
  peeled and de-veined
2 pheasant breasts, skin removed
30 tarragon leaves

Sauce

50 ml fresh tomato purée
  (see page 221)
juice of ½ lemon
1 teaspoon English mustard

pinch of sugar
300 ml crème fraîche
salt
white pepper

Garnish

6 mustard green stems or hearts

Timbales

Gently heat the consommé for later use. Place the dariole moulds in the fridge to cool while preparing the contents.

Remove the core from the tomatoes and cut a cross into the skin. Blanch the tomatoes for 10–15 seconds, and then refresh in iced water. Peel, seed, cut into cubes, and set aside.

Boil quail eggs for about 5 minutes, refresh and peel, cut in halves.

Fry the abalone mushrooms quickly on both sides in the olive oil and season with salt and pepper. Set aside on kitchen paper to drain.

Slice the pickled ginger into a fine julienne. Dip the prawns and pheasant breasts into boiling water and then into iced water. Steep both in a third of the chicken consommé until cooked. Cool, and slice into pieces large enough for the timbale.

Spoon some of the remaining consommé into the moulds and swirl to line the mould. Chill. Repeat the chilling–lining process until the thickness of the lining is about 2–3 mm evenly around the mould then return to the fridge and let the consommé set. Once firm, place a layer of whole tarragon leaves in each mould, and layer the quail eggs, ginger, pheasant, prawns and half the tomato cubes on top. Reserve the remaining tomato cubes for garnish. Chop 10 tarragon leaves. Add the chopped tarragon to the remaining consommé and pour into the moulds until full. Return the moulds to the fridge and let the timbales set overnight, or for at least 2 hours.

Sauce

Mix the tomato purée, lemon juice, English mustard and sugar with crème fraîche and adjust seasoning.

Garnish

Blanch mustard green stems or hearts.

Composition

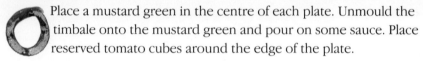 Place a mustard green in the centre of each plate. Unmould the timbale onto the mustard green and pour on some sauce. Place reserved tomato cubes around the edge of the plate.

Spicy calamari with swamp cabbage and chilli hoi sin sauce

I remember a day at BB Park in Kuala Lumpur. It has a fun fair, with a roller coaster, an outdoor cinema where avid watchers line rows of benches, and of course plenty of hawker cuisine. The stalls offer many different varieties of food, but the theme is simple. It is food to be picked up, like capsicum pieces stuffed with fishball mixture, or with bean curd, and brandished on satay sticks. There are no niceties here, just sheer greedy fun—this is old-style takeaway. The atmosphere is one of a carnival—the squid is the dish I like most...

My dad used to stand behind us in the kitchen at Neddy's and give us advice. He reminded me of this visit when I was cooking calamari and suggested using the local southern squid rather than the dried reconstituted arrowhead which is traditional in Malaysia. Our southern variety is perfect for this dish—even Malaysian purists would agree, I am sure. It was on the entrée list at Neddy's for years and was well received by guests who had a yen for spiciness.

Traditionally served with kangkong (swamp cabbage), this hawker-style dish is great for seafood lovers. Matching flavours is the European way, so this dish is not European. The Mediterranean 'big flavoured' style is as close as the West comes to this style. One piece of dried chilli is necessary to put some heat into the oil and to give it a slightly spicy flavour. The sauce is actually a three-in-one—as tricky as a sideshow.

In Asia the dried calamari is soaked in lye (alkaline) water which is changed several times until the calamari swells to its original size. In Australia we are fortunate to find fresh, succulent calamari in abundance, which is larger than the Asian variety (cuttlefish can also be used). Try to avoid cleaning the calamari (or indeed any fresh seafood) under running cold water—it reduces the intensity of the flavour. If the calamari needs any cleaning, gently wipe the surface with a damp towel or kitchen paper.

Swamp cabbage and calamari

2 bunches swamp cabbage
  (kangkong)
salt
1 clove garlic, chopped

2 whole calamari (squid)
2 tablespoons peanut oil
2 whole shallots
1 slice ginger, finely chopped

Sauce

1 tablespoon peanut oil
½ tablespoon fermented
  brown bean paste
1 clove chopped garlic
1 knob chopped ginger
½ tablespoon fermented
  white bean curd

2 tablespoons vinegar chilli sauce
⅓ cup hoi sin sauce
3 tablespoons water
2 tablespoons sugar
1 teaspoon English mustard powder
½ teaspoon lemon juice

Garnish

toasted sesame seeds

Swamp cabbage and calamari

Wash the swamp cabbage thoroughly, gathering all the stems together. Cut off any hard, woody stems. Cut the cabbage into 6 cm long pieces, keeping the stem separate from the leaves.

Bring some water to the boil in a saucepan or wok, and add a pinch of salt and chopped garlic. Put in the cabbage stems and cook for a couple of minutes. Add leaves and cook for 1 minute longer.

Strain the swamp cabbage in a colander, let it stand for a few minutes and shake off any excess water. Set aside on a plate.

Remove the calamari innards by gently pulling the head and tentacles, trying to keep the intestinal sac intact. Reserve the tentacles for frying with body meat. Wipe over the internal and external surfaces of the calamari with a damp cloth or kitchen paper. Peel off the purplish membrane, starting from the wing. Cut the calamari in half lengthways. With the skin facing down, slice each piece, at an angle of 65°, into 2 cm x 5 cm pieces, lifting the flesh away from the skin as you cut.

Heat oil in a frying-pan. Add shallots, ginger, a little salt and calamari. Sauté for 1 minute, ensuring you do not overcook. Strain in a colander.

Sauce

In a saucepan heat the oil. Add the brown bean paste, garlic and ginger, and fry for a few seconds. Add white fermented bean curd and the chilli sauce, and then add hoi sin sauce and water and bring to the boil. Add the sugar. Mix the mustard powder with a little extra water and the lemon juice and stir into the bean mixture.

Composition

 Place swamp cabbage on individual plates and sautéed calamari on the cabbage. Spoon as much sauce as you like over the calamari. Garnish with toasted sesame seeds.

Shark lips, scallops and sea cucumber braised in carrot oil

In 1984, George Orwell's famous year, Mary, Eugenia (8 months old) and I are in Beijing. Our first eating experience is sea cucumber, then sea cucumber, then more sea cucumber, Shandong style. While in Beijing we are treated to the tourist circuit by my maternal uncle. Working for a computer company he is always properly attired in the Chinese grey suit, telling friends and acquaintances about his visitors from the Golden Mountain—the description of Australia in the gold-rush days. In Bee Hai Park, in the heart of Beijing, we see people digging up lotus roots from the partially drained lake, and selling them on the bridge. We are on our way to lunch at one of the best-known Beijing restaurants, called Fanshan, or the Emperor's Kitchen.

At Fanshan, the food is presented in the traditional banquet style. I am eating a fantastic dish of pure white asparagus with scallops which have been braised with roasted garlic. Then there's Buddha's hand—a sweet paste enclosed in layered pastry. A magnificent sweet snow-pea cake is presented as a perfect square-based pyramid—reminiscent of the Japanese-style of presentation. As soon as the chopsticks hit the pyramid it gently falls, rather like brushing a mound of feathers. A trestle of bean sprouts, topped and tailed and mounded, is another memorable dish. There is a corn dumpling dish, described as a spearhead, and chestnut dumplings, too—another marvellous eating experience. And then come the sliced fish dishes and the inevitable braised sea cucumber.

When I came home to Neddy's I was very interested in preparing this sea cucumber dish because it looked European in style. I had bought the Fanshan recipe book, written entirely in Chinese, which I cannot read. At least there were illustrations. I asked my mother to read out the recipe to me and as my family had experience in handling all the dry ingredients it contained, such as shark lips and sea cucumber, it was one I was confident of being able to do properly.

A particular variety of sea cucumber, found in the north, is called little sow piglet, because it is no longer than 8 centimetres and has little outgrowths, like nipples. Eating this variety is very different from eating southern varieties. It is crunchy and crisp like cucumber, not gelatinous and sloppy.

Use a good quality soy sauce for this dish at all times if you can. I define good quality light grade soy sauce as one which has a slightly alcoholic taste, and is not too salty. First grade soy sauce could be obtained from vats when I lived in Malaysia; unlike the commercial varieties, it did not have a long shelf life. From those available in Australia, the one I like the most is the Tinsong Tin label, which translates as 'Heaven above Heaven', made in Malaysia and slightly more expensive than most. It is also superior to any commercial Japanese type I have tried.

A signature Neddy's dish, resplendent in fragrant orange-red carrot oil. The carrot oil is made by cooking grated carrot very slowly in peanut oil, until the rich red colour emerges. The dried shiitake mushrooms give a richer flavour than the fresh variety, so do not fall into the trap of thinking that fresh is best in this case. Doused in rice wine and flamed, there is drama and heat to balance the Yin, or cool, elements of shark lips and sea cucumber. The cucumber requires soaking for three days in advance so plan well ahead. There should be just enough liquid to coat the contents—the dish should not be swimming in sauce.

Sea cucumber

200 g sea cucumber, soaked
  for 3 days, changing the
  water every day
2 large slices ginger
1 spring onion

250 ml white chicken stock
  (see page 224)
2 tablespoons yellow rice wine,
  Shaoshing variety
pinch of salt

Shark lips

150 g shark lips, soaked for
  6 hours in cold water
4 slices ginger
2 spring onions

200 ml white chicken stock
  (see page 224)
pinch of salt
2 tablespoons yellow rice wine

Scallops

50 g scallops
½ teaspoon ginger juice

½ teaspoon shallot juice

Vegetables

3 tablespoons carrot oil
8 slices winter bamboo shoots,
  tinned Maling brand
6 whole Chinese mushrooms,
  pre-soaked
1 teaspoon finely chopped garlic
1 teaspoon finely chopped ginger
½ tablespoon finely chopped
  shallots

1 dried chilli
8 strips carrot,
  1 cm x 5 cm x 3 mm thick
2 tablespoons rice wine
2 tablespoons light soy sauce
½ tablespoon oyster sauce
50 g sugar

Garnish

celery leaves, deep-fried in oil

julienne of carrots

Sea cucumber

Scrub off all the white lime from the soaked sea cucumber. Remove the
innards and all sand thoroughly. Put the sea cucumber in a saucepan and
cover with cold water. Add the slices of ginger and spring onion and
simmer for 1 hour.

Strain and refresh sea cucumber in cold water and thoroughly clean it
again. Put clean cucumber in a bowl, add chicken stock, rice wine and salt
and put the bowl in a steamer and steam for a further 1 hour until tender.
It is now ready for use.

Shark lips

Scrape the sandy skin off the soaked shark lips, then cut into pieces 3–4 cm long.

In a saucepan, place 2 slices of ginger, 1 spring onion and some cold water, and bring to the boil. Blanch the shark lips and refresh in cold water.

Add the shark lips to the chicken stock, remaining ginger, spring onion, salt and rice wine and steam for 10 minutes. (Thicker shark lips may need to steam for up to 20 minutes until soft.)

Scallops

Remove the coral and the outer black sac from the scallops. Season with ginger and shallot juice.

Vegetables

Heat up the carrot oil (see page 31) and add the bamboo shoots and Chinese mushrooms. Then add the garlic, ginger, shallots and dried chilli, and fry until fragrant. Add the scallops, sliced carrot, sea cucumber and shark lips and fry for 2 minutes. Add in rice wine, soy sauce, oyster sauce and sugar. Cook until the sauce has reduced to a coating consistency and the oil separates from the liquid.

Composition

 Place on individual plates and garnish with deep-fried celery leaves and julienne of carrots.

Kangaroo fillet, veal tongue and braised witlof

Neddy's was among the first restaurants to serve kangaroo. It took a few weeks to perfect the technique—we experimented with stir-fry and braising—but finally we grilled it rare. This was the best method because the meat is so lean and lacks a distinct game flavour. It has a slightly coarser grain compared with venison and tends to lose fluid as soon as it is cooked. Eating it rare is an excellent way to enjoy the delicate flavour and velvety texture of the meat. This particular dish reflects the Alsace tradition of serving meat with mustard and veal tongue. The tongue, being very well cooked and moistened with gelatine from the pork fat rind, provides a contrast to the bleu style of the kangaroo. The witlof imparts an earthy, slightly bitter flavour.

This dish was created in the late 1970s when kangaroo was first introduced for human consumption in South Australia, the first state in Australia to do so. Jesser Meat, originally a pet-food processor, supplied the meat. You can use kangaroo meat as a substitute for venison but choose dishes that are pan fried or grilled. Generally kangaroo can be used for Asian stir-fry but the meat needs to be sliced more thickly to keep it rare, which is not strictly *de rigueur*.

Kangaroo fillet
1 kg kangaroo loin fillet, trimmed
salt
freshly ground black pepper
1 tablespoon olive oil

80 g butter
450 g witlof
1 teaspoon lemon juice
⅓ cup mineral water

Sauce
350 ml kangaroo stock
  (see page 228)
⅓ cup dry white wine
1 egg yolk

300 ml crème fraîche
4 tablespoons Dijon mustard
50 g butter, cubed

Veal tongues
6 veal tongues
200 g pork rind, blanched
500 ml brown veal stock
  (see page 226)

250 ml dry white wine
1 carrot, thickly sliced
1 onion, roughly sliced
bouquet garni

Garnish
baby gherkins

Kangaroo fillet

Preheat the oven to 160°C. Cut the kangaroo loin into 6 equal portions. Season with salt and pepper. Heat the oil and add a third of the butter. When it foams, seal the meat on all sides and then place it in the oven for 20 minutes. Remove and allow to rest in a warm place.

Wash the witlof in running water, and trim. Do not stand it in water as it will become bitter. Add remaining butter to a saucepan, sprinkle with salt, then add lemon juice and witlof. Baste the witlof, then add the mineral water (mineral water is cleaner than tap water). Place in an ovenproof dish, cover with buttered paper and then the lid, and cook in the oven at 160°C for 40 minutes.

Sauce

Prepare the sauce by combining stock and wine in a saucepan and reducing by two-thirds. Whisk egg yolk and crème fraîche together and then add to the reduced stock. Lower the heat to medium. Drain the braised witlof, add to the sauce then stir in the mustard until the sauce is smooth. Stir in butter cubes.

Veal tongues

Place tongues in a saucepan with the blanched pork rind. Cover with cold water and bring to the boil for 10 minutes. Remove tongues with a slotted spoon and plunge into cold water. Peel the skin off the tongues and cut off the meaty portion towards the back. Add the white wine, carrot, onion and bouquet garni to the veal stock and bring back to the boil. Add the tongues and simmer for 1½ hours. Allow tongues to cool in the stock.

Composition

Arrange braised witlof on a plate along with the slices of kangaroo fillet, which should be pink in colour, and slices of the tongue. Spoon the sauce around the meat and garnish with baby gherkins.

Roast suckling pig with green ginger wine and spiced spinach purée

I've tried many European-style whole pigs, but it is a quite different experience to eat a whole Chinese suckling pig. Traditionally, the pig is first split in half along the back, leaving the breast intact. It is coated with maltose and vinegar and left to hang to dry in front of a fan for at least 6 to 8 hours. The skin is stretched at this stage, using long pieces of wood inside the pig. The Chinese like to roast the crackling first over charcoal. The pig is then turned to cook the meat and once done, the skin is finished off over the fine embers. There are no bubbles in the skin—the crackling is thin and biscuit-like. In this recipe I have adapted the Chinese method to suit the limitations of a domestic stove.

I used ginger wine and honey because I once drank a combination of rum and Stone's Green Ginger Wine with Barry Ross at a pub in the Adelaide Hills, on a very cold night. It convinced me that Australian ginger wine deserved a place in my dishes, instead of rice wine. So we basted the pig with honey and ginger wine and it worked well.

The spinach purée is classical Indian—blanched, puréed and sieved to a smooth texture. It is then combined with Indian spices and braised to create a delicious and creamy vegetable accompaniment to the suckling pig.

Most of the effort in the Chinese method of cooking suckling pig is directed at perfecting the thin crunchiness of the skin, which is highly prized; the meat is just a bonus.

Roast suckling pig

7 kg suckling pig
150 g salt
olive oil

750 g mirepoix of onion, carrots, celery
300 ml green ginger wine
40 ml honey

Spicy spinach purée

3 bunches Valita spinach
2 tablespoons butter
1 teaspoon poppy seeds
1 teaspoon black mustard seeds
1 teaspoon freshly crushed cumin
1 teaspoon freshly ground
  black pepper

½ tablespoon chopped garlic
2 tablespoons ground fresh ginger
100 g finely chopped shallots
1 medium tomato, skinned,
  seeded and diced
salt

Garnish
glacé ginger, sliced

Roast suckling pig

Preheat the oven to 280°C. Wipe the whole suckling pig clean and rub with salt. Lightly score the skin and brush lightly with olive oil. Place some mirepoix on the base of a roasting dish and put the pig on top.

Put the suckling pig in the oven and turn down the temperature to 220°C and cook for 30 minutes. Baste with olive oil then turn the temperature to 180°C and cook for a further hour, basting again after 30 minutes. Cook for longer of course if the pig is larger than 7 kg.

Mix the green ginger wine and honey together. Take the roasting dish from the oven and remove all the fat from the dish before pouring the green ginger wine and honey over the pork. Cook for a further 30 minutes.

Spicy spinach purée

Wash spinach thoroughly to remove all sand and dirt. Blanch in hot salted water, then purée. In a large heavy pot, heat the butter until it starts to foam. Add the poppy seeds, mustard seeds, cumin and black pepper. Sauté until the seeds begin to pop. Add the garlic, ginger, shallots and tomato and cook for a few minutes. Add the spinach purée and cook gently at a very low heat for 5 minutes. Season with salt.

Composition

Remove the crispy skin from the pig and cut the pork meat and skin into 5 cm x 8 cm cubes. Spoon purée into the centre of individual plates and add two pieces of pork then spoon over the roasting juice. Place two pieces of crackling on top and garnish with sliced glacé ginger.

Anise and ginger flavoured duck with steamed lotus bun

This is country-style cuisine at its best, showing the effects of affluence and good harvests upon simple peasant life. The bun resembles the shape of half-closed lotus leaves, hence the name. The northern Chinese use bread or buns rather than rice as an accompaniment.

Thoroughly tender, rich, mahogany-coloured glazed pieces of duck, exuding an enticing aroma of anise, is what you should be aiming for in this dish. Traditionally the skin is left on, but those who are very fat-conscious could remove it before cooking. Alternatively and preferably, try scoring the skin and fat before frying; this will tend to reduce the amount of fat. If you don't want to make the lotus bun, serve it with plenty of boiled white rice. Crisply sautéed red and green capsicum adds a crunchy and colourful touch to the dish.

Duck

1.2 kg duck
250 ml peanut oil
60 ml sesame oil
2 star anise
2 dried chillies, chopped
1 tablespoon spring onion,
  white only, chopped
½ cup sliced ginger

3 cloves garlic, sliced
60 ml yellow rice wine
1½ cups white chicken stock
  (see page 224)
250 ml dark soy sauce
40 g rock sugar, crushed
1 large red capsicum
1 large green capsicum

Steamed lotus buns

1 eggwhite
1 teaspoon ammonium carbonate
⅔ cup water
320 g crumpet flour
80 g sugar
1 tablespoon lard

2 teaspoons baking powder,
  double-action variety
600 g sourdough (see page 229)
1 teaspoon lye water
sesame oil

Duck

Cut duck into 6 large pieces, without de-boning. Score skin and fat in a diamond pattern. Heat almost all the oil and fry duck pieces until golden on all sides. Remove duck pieces and place on kitchen paper in a warm place. In a heavy pot, heat sesame oil with star anise, dried chillies, spring onion, sliced ginger, and garlic then stir and fry until it smokes. Add duck. Flame with rice wine, cook off the alcohol, then add stock, soy sauce and bring to the boil. Skim off the residue, then simmer for about 1 hour. The meat is ready when it pulls away from the bone easily; the juice should be reduced by two-thirds. At the last minute add rock sugar (otherwise it turns sour) and cook until the meat is glazed.

Cut capsicum into 3 cm triangles. Heat the remaining peanut oil in a frying-pan and lightly sauté the capsicum, adding duck and juices for the last 5 minutes. Skim the fat off the juice and pour over the duck before serving.

Steamed lotus buns

Mix eggwhite, ammonium carbonate and water. Combine flour, sugar, lard and baking powder with the liquid and mix to soft dough stage. To neutralise the acidity of the sourdough, add lye water. Mix both doughs together and knead until glossy. Take half the dough and roll into a log about 3 cm in diameter. Divide into 6 cm long pieces, or three finger lengths as the Chinese say. Roll each piece into a ball and flatten to form a disc about 6 cm in diameter. Lightly brush with the sesame oil and fold in half to form a half-moon shape. Holding the dough with three fingers, use the back of the knife to gather up the pastry and push it up through the joining skin of the fingers to create two sets of gathers. This method ensures an even size and can be applied to other bread rolls.

Place on a lightly oiled plate. Repeat the process with the rest of the dough and steam for 10 minutes (the dough does not need proving).

Rhubarb tart with clove cream and chocolate figs

Chocolate figs were the sweet standby at Neddy's. We kept them in jars ready to add to a dish or to be served on their own with coffee to those guests who were not keen on a full-size dessert. They are a great accompaniment to rhubarb, with its slightly tangy flavour.

Rhubarb should be obtained from a good greengrocer and used on the day it has been cut to get the full flavour and to ensure crispness. It is best picked early in the day if you have your own supply.

One of the secrets of this dish is to cook the rhubarb in the liquid, then reduce that liquid to syrup. This gives colour and flavour to the dish and ensures that the syrup is not watery and the rhubarb is not overcooked.

Rhubarb compôte
500 g rhubarb
3 tablespoons unsalted butter
125 g pure icing sugar

2 cm knob ginger, cut into very
  fine strips

Crumble and pastry
100 g almonds
100 g pure icing sugar
100 g unsalted butter
100 g flour

sweet-crust pastry
  (see page 231)
six 8 cm flan tins

Chocolate figs
300 g dried figs
250 g bitter chocolate, grated

100 g almonds
300 ml white port

Clove cream
100 ml crème fraîche   *2 whole cloves, finely ground*

Rhubarb compôte

Skin the rhubarb and cut into 4 cm sticks, reserving the skin. Melt the butter with the icing sugar until it begins to foam then add in the rhubarb skin to give the compôte its colour. Cook until the juice emerges then strain the liquid. Discard the rhubarb skin. Put the liquid back into the pot and add the ginger and the rhubarb pieces. Bring to the boil, turn off the heat and allow to sit for 10 minutes. The fruit should be soft but not over-cooked. Drain off the juice and reduce it to a syrup. Add the syrup back to the rhubarb compôte.

Crumble and pastry

Grind almonds into meal, then toast until golden. Rub together toasted almond meal, icing sugar, butter and flour.

Preheat the oven to 190°C. Line the tins with sweet pastry and blind bake for 20 minutes. Remove foil and pulses and fill flans with warm rhubarb compôte. Lightly cover the compôte with the crumble and bake in the oven for a further 7 minutes until light brown. Time the completion of the tart so that it can be served immediately with the cream and figs.

Chocolate figs

Puff up the dried figs by pulling the tip and the base of the figs out. Reshape using your finger through the base of the fig, creating an opening. Grind almonds into meal, then toast until golden. Mix 100 g of the bitter chocolate with the almond meal. Fill the figs with the almond meal mixture and close the opening. Place in a saucepan and cover with white port. Add the rest of the chocolate. Do not boil the mixture, just let it simmer in the saucepan until the liquid is reduced by half.

Clove cream

Whip crème fraîche to a soft peak then fold in the cloves.

Composition

Place the tart in the centre of the plate. Place the figs at the side of the plate next to the tart. Pipe the clove cream on top of the crumble and serve immediately.

Black rice and palm sugar pudding

This dish was created by Mary when she discovered the Ceylonese palm sugar custard. She decided to add black rice to the custard and I suggested we should make it nonya style—like a custard cake—with the rice layered in the centre. The dish became a legend; it is a tribute to her that so many have adapted it for their own menus.

The colour scheme of this dessert is very subtle, with hues of dark cream, brown and black, and it has overtones of a crème caramel but with a much more intense flavour. The eating experience is exquisite—it melts in the mouth and each spoonful is to be treasured. The nutty flavour and texture of the rice blends beautifully with the soft custard, and the roasted pear garnish complements both. The rice and the caramel can be prepared in advance for this dish.

Black rice
150 g black rice
300 ml water

pinch of salt

Caramel
200 g castor sugar

100 ml water

Custard
1 litre milk
200 g desiccated coconut
150 g palm sugar

4 eggs
8 egg yolks

Garnish
6 pears
1 litre stock syrup
   (see page 232)

1 vanilla bean
icing sugar for dusting

Black rice

Add the black rice to the water with the salt. Bring to the boil, reduce to a simmer and cook until tender (rice splits open).

Caramel

Mix sugar and water together over a medium heat to make a dark caramel. Remove from the heat as soon as it turns brown; it will keep cooking away from the heat. Don't stir, but brush the sides of the pot with cold water to incorporate all the sugar. If you would like it a little browner, put it back over the heat. Clean and lightly oil a mould and line with the caramel. Allow to cool. The remaining caramel becomes the pouring sauce: to prevent it from setting, dilute with water until the caramel has the consistency of sauce.

Custard

Preheat the oven to 150°C. Scald the milk and add the desiccated coconut and palm sugar and allow to stand for 30 minutes before straining. Lightly beat together the eggs and egg yolks. Pour the warm milk into the eggs. Pour half this mixture into the mould and cook in a bain-marie in the oven. Just before it is completely set (about 30 minutes), add a layer of black rice and then another layer of the custard mixture. Cook until set—about 40 minutes. Chill in the fridge.

Garnish

Poach the pears in the stock syrup with the vanilla bean. When cooked, slice each pear into 4 pieces, retaining the pear shape. Dust with icing sugar and place in a hot oven until caramelised.

Composition

 Unmould the custard by submerging the mould in warm water. Carefully turn the mould out onto a serving plate. Pour over a little diluted caramel sauce and serve with a roasted pear.

Adelaide Courtyard

When we were designing a new menu the courtyard at Neddy's often gave us inspiration. We could have been anywhere. We dreamed in the Land of the Dreaming as my good friend John Ho said, and the courtyard led us to the Middle East along the spice routes, to the Greek Islands, to Tuscany, Provence, Singapore, Sichuan and last but not least to the Australian back garden.

Neddy's was *the* courtyard restaurant in summer. People inside fought for an outside table and if one became free there would be a swift exodus. It was urbane or homely depending on your needs—you could breastfeed there, or play politics, or both. Australian bluestone lined the walls giving it a very provincial feel and yet the food was beyond traditions, which Australians relished.

The grapevine was gnarled and almost a century old, and the black table grapes were often used for a garnish or soaked in brandy, frozen, dusted with icing sugar, and served with cheese. The grapevine went well with the long winemakers' lunches. Serious drinkers like Philip White, Howard Twelftree and Len Evans came often; others were Geoff Merrill, Chris Hackett, Brian Croser, Martin Smith, Wolf Blass, Bob McLean, Robert O'Callaghan, Tim Knappstein, Adam and David Wynn, Michel Dietrich, Tom Hardy and many more.

Among the memorable interstate visitors were the big personalities like

Barry Humphries, Adelaide Festival heavies such as Jim Sharman, authors V. S. Naipaul and Patrick White, actors Edward Woodward, David Hemmings, Bryan Brown, Rachel Ward, Derek Nimmo, Jack Thompson, and Diana Rigg; from the musical scene, John Martin the folk guitarist and Neil Sedaka, and artists Lloyd Rees and John Olsen. Being Australian we have to mention the sporting life—Ian Botham came in, hoping for the Ashes on a plate. As for the inevitable 'politerati', the Whitlams were among them.

Leaving the glamour aside, we often kept live chickens in the cellar for a day before killing them, and our pigeons were housed at the back— both highly illegal practices. Australia's health regulations work against the absolute freshness which, as the Chinese know, a really good poultry dish needs. Few of our customers were aware of quite *how* fresh their ingredients really were—killings were ritually performed after lunch and new apprentices turned green at the sight of a pigeon sacrifice.

Christmas in the courtyard was celebrated at the long table—friends and relatives gathered and it was a time for the staff to relax and enjoy the courtyard and the friendship.

Neddy's courtyard was atmospheric, reflecting the multicultural mood of Australia in the 1970s. There were the aromas of Chinese pork and European venison, the romance of provincial France in the stone walls, and the bouquet of big Australian reds, such as Wendouree from the gentle Clare Valley in South Australia. The following menu captures the memory of warm nights and seductive food under the vines.

Adelaide Courtyard recipes

LAMB SAHARA
WITH NAAN BREAD

ORANGE AND HONEYDEW
GRENADINE SALAD

GARLIC PÂTÉ
WITH GRILLED BREAD

POT-ROASTED PIGEON WITH GARLIC
AND GRILLED FIGS

GRILLED RED MULLET WITH LEMON,
CHILLI AND MARJORAM

WARM SALAD OF SHIITAKE AND ABALONE MUSHROOMS
WITH PASTA

CABBAGE SALAD
WITH SPICED SWEET TOMATO DRESSING

CUCUMBER AND BITTER GREEN SALAD
WITH LIME DRESSING

DEEP-FRIED MUSSELS
IN SOFT BATTER

KANGAROO MOROCCAN STYLE WITH COUSCOUS
AND CHICK PEAS

WHITE PORK SLICES
WITH GARLIC SAUCE

CHINESE SHORTCAKE
SERVED WITH JASMINE TEA

Lamb Sahara with naan bread

Eating fish led to this dish—a spiced fish with chilli and tahini—rich, fragrant, addictive and romantic.

This is a Middle-Eastern-style dish that relies on a combination of olives, chilli, pinenuts, tahini and sugar to enhance the lamb, giving it a nutty sweetness and well marinated flavour. The dish would please a Bedouin or a Hakka. Hakka ('guests' in Chinese) belong to the nomadic Chinese dialect group which moved for centuries from north to south China and who have now wandered into this ancient continent (along with the other 17 million or so Australian guests).

Naan bread can be prepared in advance. Using yoghurt gives a slightly tangy flavour.

Marinade

1 tablespoon Worcestershire sauce
pinch of cayenne pepper
1 teaspoon paprika
1 clove garlic, finely chopped
1 tablespoon white wine
1 tablespoon dark soy sauce

2 stalks dried marjoram
1 teaspoon ground cinnamon
1 tablespoon vinegar
pinch of salt and freshly
   ground black pepper

Lamb Sahara

500 g boneless lamb loin cut
   into 1 cm cubes
2½ tablespoons olive oil
3 cloves garlic, chopped
1 tablespoon chopped shallots
1 carrot cut into 2 cm x 1 cm strips
12 small pickled chillies,
   Lebanese style
1 tablespoon black olives cut
   into slivers

1 teaspoon lemon zest
2 teaspoons sugar
2 tablespoons tahini
2 stalks dried marjoram
juice of ½ lemon
1 tablespoon roasted pinenuts
½ red capsicum, cut into
   1 cm x 1 cm cubes

Naan bread

800 g plain flour	2 eggs
1 tablespoon sugar	225 ml milk (or ½ milk,
1 teaspoon baking powder	½ yoghurt)
1 scant teaspoon bicarb soda	1½ tablespoons unsalted
½ teaspoon salt	butter, melted

Garnish

fresh mint, coriander or parsley

Marinade

Mix all ingredients together. Add lamb cubes and marinate for at least 30 minutes.

Lamb Sahara

Preheat the oven to 220°C. Remove the lamb from the marinade and place on kitchen paper to absorb excess liquid. Heat the oil in a heavy skillet until it begins to smoke and then add the garlic, shallots and lamb cubes. Brown the lamb quickly, stirring it, then add the carrots and pickled chillies, olives, lemon zest and sugar. Stir in the tahini and crumbled dried marjoram.

Place the lamb in a baking dish and bake in the oven for 20 minutes, after which the lamb should have a nice crust. Squeeze lemon juice over the lamb and allow to rest outside the oven for a few minutes. When the oil exudes from the meat, sprinkle the roasted pinenuts and capsicum cubes over the top and return the dish to the oven for a further 2 minutes.

Naan bread

Preheat the oven to 190°C. Sift together the dry ingredients. Whisk the eggs with the milk and melted butter. Form a well in the flour mixture and slowly add the egg and milk mixture to form a soft dough. Divide into 6 pieces of dough. Roll out each piece and shape it to resemble the palm of a hand. Place dough on a baking tray lined with baking paper or use a baking stone. Bake for 8 minutes then remove them.

Composition

Serve the bread on a separate platter. Place the lamb pieces on a second platter and garnish with fresh herbs such as mint, coriander and parsley. You can split the bread and place the meat inside if you want to vary this presentation.

Orange and honeydew grenadine salad

Adapted some years ago from a recipe in a Middle Eastern cookbook and very exotic in both colour and taste. Add pomegranate seeds if you can get them. They are like nectar and the rose colour is superb. Use the melon shell to serve this salad.

4 large oranges	3 tablespoons grenadine syrup
2 pink grapefruit	¼ cup chopped fresh mint
½ pineapple, cubed	pinch of saffron
120 ml Cointreau	1 ripe honeydew melon

To seed and fillet the oranges and grapefruit, first peel the skin and membrane off both. Using a sharp knife, cut down one side of the membrane between each segment and flip the segment out, removing the seeds at the same time. Macerate the orange, grapefruit and pineapple in the Cointreau and grenadine syrup and add the mint and saffron. Refrigerate for 1 hour.

Cut the melon in half lengthwise and using a ball scoop, make melon balls. Mix with the macerated fruits (adding the melon at this second stage preserves the colour contrast). Using a spoon, remove any remaining flesh from the melon shell and discard it.

Composition

Fill the shell with the macerated fruit and serve.

Garlic pâté with grilled bread

This is not my own invention. It belongs to Mediterranean and Arabic peoples and can be found throughout the region in all its guises. I chose it because it makes a perfect courtyard dish and, with a good bread to accompany it, is a simple delight.

One of those perennial dishes that is passed down within cultures and across cultures. Fresh, good-quality garlic and perfect brie are mandatory. Both can be found locally: certain Australian cheesemakers produce excellent bries.

Garlic pâté
2 large whole garlic bulbs
¼ cold, ripe brie, trimmed
  of white rind, then cut into
  2 cm cubes

1 teaspoon cayenne pepper
750 ml olive oil
1 cup hot water

Grilled bread
French stick
good quality virgin olive oil

Garlic pâté

Preheat the oven to a slow 150°C. Bundle the whole, unpeeled bulbs of garlic in a double thickness of aluminium foil, then twist each loose end into a gooseneck to seal. Place in the oven and roast for 1 hour then remove and cool to room temperature. Place the brie in the top of a double-boiler set over simmering water and allow to soften for 8–10 minutes (do not allow the water to boil or the cheese may string and separate). Meanwhile, peel the garlic clove by clove and drop into an electric blender or a food processor fitted with a metal chopping blade. Add the cayenne pepper, olive oil and hot water and buzz for 30 seconds non-stop to purée. Scrape down the sides of the blender and buzz for 30 seconds longer. Now add the softened cheese and incorporate, using 8–10 quick on-offs of the motor. Transfer to a small bowl and, if the mixture seems slightly lumpy, whisk hard by hand (further machine-beating at this point may make the pâté rubbery). Store in an airtight container in the refrigerator. Bring to room temperature before serving.

Grilled bread

Brush slices of French stick with the olive oil and grill until light brown.

Composition

 Place pâté in the centre of a large plate and put bread around the edge of the plate.

Pot-roasted pigeon with garlic and grilled figs

I first learnt how to cook pot-roasted pigeon from a Greek chef who used a combination of walnuts, brandy and cream. The Tuscan style of pot roasting—lots of garlic and lightly crumbed with Parmesan and breadcrumbs—makes the dish less rich. Just when you thought it might be entirely Mediterranean I add the curry for piquancy. I once stacked 80 pigeons into a pyramid studded with figs and surrounded it with lemon wedges—it's a courtyard platter dish after all.

This dish is an alfresco delight. If you are not quite ready to tackle a pyramid, then simply serve the pigeon with ribbon pasta or rice, or with the figs and salad. Adelaide's Mediterranean climate produces the blackest and nicest of figs to accompany this dish, so look for the best quality in your corner of the globe—new-season figs are the best.

Pot-roasted pigeon

6 pigeons

3 teaspoons salt

3 teaspoons freshly ground
   black pepper

6 whole garlic bulbs

12 cloves

6 spring onions

zest of 1 lemon

1 stick cinnamon, broken
   into 6 pieces

4 tablespoons olive oil

170 g butter

1 bay leaf

6 cardamom pods

3 tablespoons brandy

½ cup white wine

500 ml white chicken stock
   (see page 224)

100 g Parmesan cheese

1 tablespoon Madras curry powder

1 teaspoon cayenne pepper

50 g white breadcrumbs

Grilled figs

6 fresh figs

olive oil

icing sugar

freshly ground black pepper

Garnish

lemon wedges

Pot-roasted pigeon

Preheat the oven to 180°C. Season each pigeon with half a teaspoon of the salt and pepper, rubbing it thoroughly within the cavity and on the skin.

Let it stand for 30 minutes.

Put 2 garlic cloves and 2 cloves, 1 spring onion, some lemon zest and 1 piece of cinnamon stick in the cavity of each bird.

In a heavy-based ovenproof pot, heat the olive oil then add 50 g of the butter and brown each pigeon. Slice the remaining whole garlic bulbs in half horizontally. Add the garlic, bay leaf and cardamom pods and sauté for a few minutes. Then pour in the brandy and flame. Add white wine, reduce, then add chicken stock and bring to the boil. Place the pot in the oven and cook until pigeons are tender, basting every 20 minutes.

Once tender, remove the pot from the oven and allow the pigeons to cool in the jus. When cool, remove from the jus and lightly dust each bird with Parmesan cheese, curry powder and cayenne pepper then breadcrumbs. Melt the remaining butter and pour some over each pigeon. Place the pigeons in a clean pan with some of the jus from the pot-roasting pan and brown in the oven.

Grilled figs

Halve the figs, brush with a little oil and dust with a little icing sugar and black pepper. Place cut-side down on a metal tray. Bake in oven, or grill, until caramelised.

Composition

 Serve the pigeons with the warm grilled figs and fresh lemon. Spoon the remaining jus over the pigeons.

Grilled red mullet with lemon, chilli and marjoram

I discovered red mullet when I was cooking at the Iliad restaurant back in the early 1970s. The Greeks loved this fish, simply pan fried with lemon and garlic, and fortunately for them it was not very popular with other Australians at that time. This dish was born when a cousin visited from Toronto and I reheated this fish—normally heresy—and threw some Madras curry powder over it. The combination of the curry powder with the butter gives it a cross-cultural touch—Asia, the Middle East and the Mediterranean all in one.

Small red mullet from cold waters are the best choice, rather than the large red mullet from the north. Choose very fresh, brightly coloured fish—as the fish deteriorates it loses its colour. Mullet is considered a game fish, with a very rich flavour, and for this reason it can be successfully accompanied by a red wine. As long as it hasn't been sitting on the shelf for too long, dried marjoram has just as much flavour as fresh, but remember, it's a last-minute herb for this dish, so don't add it during cooking.

This dish can be served with a pilaf.

6 red mullet, filleted and deboned
2 tablespoons olive oil
2 cloves garlic, finely chopped
1 teaspoon Madras curry powder
1 large red chilli, seeded and
  cut into slivers
1 bay leaf
1 large onion, sliced

2 tomatoes, skinned, seeded
  and diced
2 lemons
150 g butter, melted
2 tablespoons dry white wine,
  Noilly Prat
salt
freshly ground black pepper

Garnish
chopped coriander

freshly dried marjoram

In a frying-pan, seal the red mullet fillets in olive oil, skin-side first then quickly turn over to seal flesh. Remove from the pan and set aside on a plate. Add garlic, curry powder, chilli, bay leaf, onion and tomatoes to the same frying-pan and cook gently for a few minutes without browning.

Peel the skin and membrane off the lemons. Using a sharp knife, cut down one side of the membrane between each segment and flip the segment out, removing the seeds at the same time.

Add the red mullet fillets to the frying-pan, meat-side down, then arrange lemon segments over the top and brush with the melted butter. Add wine and put frying-pan under a griller to cook for 3 minutes.

Season with salt and pepper.

Composition

Arrange the fish on a platter and garnish with chopped coriander and dried marjoram.

Warm salad of shiitake and abalone mushrooms with pasta

This dish resembles an Asian-style vegetarian dish we used to eat at a vegetarian temple in Kuala Lumpur, reminding me of my childhood. But, while there are similarities, at the temple they used a nonya curry sauce rather than a dressing. Italian-style noodles and balsamic vinegar combine with several Asian elements to give it a distinctive feel. By the way, any time you are out of meat jus, oyster sauce is a great substitute. I decided to add chilli oil to give warmth. What I like most are the different mushroom textures—any combination is fine.

A vegetable dish designed to be served warm, never cold, with the mushrooms taking pride of place and offering both richness and lightness. Abalone mushrooms and dried and fresh shiitake mushrooms can be combined for texture. Japanese enoki ('golden hair' to the Chinese) mushrooms are a great addition for colour contrast and by all means use morels if you can get them.

Dressing

2 tablespoons oyster sauce
1 tablespoon light soy sauce
1 teaspoon rose wine,
  Chinese variety
1 tablespoon sesame oil

¼ teaspoon chilli oil,
  preferably with sesame-oil base
1 teaspoon balsamic vinegar
1 tablespoon shallot oil

Pasta

300 g plain noodle dough
  (see page 230)

cornflour for dusting

Warm salad

30 g cloud-ear fungus, dried
2 pinches of salt
6 Chinese dried mushrooms
50 g abalone mushrooms
50 g shiitake mushrooms, fresh
50 g enoki mushrooms
½ Chinese white cabbage

1 tablespoon light soy sauce
1 tablespoon sake
3 tablespoons peanut oil
2 shallots, peeled and chopped
1 tablespoon finely chopped garlic
1 cos lettuce, washed and
  leaves separated

Garnish

toasted sesame seeds
finely shredded spring onion,
  white only

fresh coriander sprigs

Dressing

Mix ingredients together.

Pasta

Cut the pasta dough into 4 even pieces and using a rolling pin roll out into rectangular sheets to 1 mm thick. Use a pasta machine if you have one, or follow this hand method. Dust with cornflour and roll each sheet, from the widest end, into a tight log. Cut the log crosswise at 3 mm intervals with a very sharp knife. Dust each piece with cornflour and using a Japanese (pointed) chopstick, 'tease' or loosen the pasta. Unravel each piece to produce your own spaghetti. Always dust the pasta with cornflour or rice flour at each step. Blanch the pasta in salted boiling water then refresh under cold water to stop the cooking process and to remove starch. Set aside.

Warm salad

Cloud-ear fungus: Put in a pot of water and bring to the boil for a few minutes then rinse in cold water, removing any twigs, stones and hard bits. Place in a pot of clean water with a pinch of salt, bring to the boil and simmer for a couple of minutes until tender.

Chinese dried mushrooms: Remove stems from dried mushrooms and discard. Put mushrooms in a pot of cold water and bring to the boil. Simmer for a few minutes then rinse and wash the mushrooms in cold water. Where the outer edge of the mushroom has curled in, open it and wash it thoroughly as this is where most dirt accumulates. Clean further by squeezing it well. Put in a fresh pot of cold water with a pinch of salt, bring to the boil and simmer until tender. Cut into strips but retain some of the juice for the later stages of cooking. This technique can be applied to all dried mushrooms.

Abalone, shiitake and enoki mushrooms: Lightly clean mushrooms with a damp cloth. Abalone mushrooms should be torn into strips and shiitake mushrooms quartered. Cut the enoki stalks away from the base.

Chinese white cabbage: Cut away the two wing leaves on either side of each stem and reserve. Cut the cabbage stem diagonally into long strips 5 mm wide. Lightly braise in soy sauce, sake and 1 tablespoon of the oil making sure the cabbage is well coated with oil.

Pasta and vegetables

In a frying-pan, heat a tablespoon of the remaining oil, add the shallots and garlic and fry until fragrant. Add the dried mushrooms, cloud ear fungus and pasta and toss over the flame until evenly cooked. Remove from the flame, pour dressing over the pasta and toss until evenly incorporated.

In a saucepan heat the remaining oil, add the salt, the shiitake, abalone and enoki mushrooms and Chinese cabbage and toss lightly. Remove from heat. Lastly, add in cos leaves.

Composition

Place the combined salad on a large plate. The pasta and mushrooms should be placed in the centre of the salad and garnished with toasted sesame seeds, shredded spring onion and coriander sprigs.

Cabbage salad with spiced sweet tomato dressing

This is the kind of salad that can successfully accompany other dishes or be served as a dish in its own right. Allow two hours for the cabbage salting–marinating process.

Salad
1 cabbage

3 tablespoons salt

Dressing
3 chillies, finely chopped
6 cloves garlic, finely chopped
1½ tablespoons finely chopped
   ginger
1 bunch coriander, finely chopped
2 tablespoons chilli sauce
   (Korean chilli paste or any
   vinegar chilli sauce)

200 ml fresh tomato purée
   (see page 221)
3 tablespoons sugar
3 tablespoons lemon juice
100 ml grapeseed oil
1 tablespoon fish sauce
1 tablespoon sesame oil

Garnish
1 tablespoon toasted sesame seeds

fresh coriander

Salad

Cut cabbage into quarters and separate the leaves. In a large bowl, knead the salt into the cabbage leaves and put a heavy weight over them, such as a plate weighted with a mortar, and stand for 2 hours.

After salting, strain off and squeeze out the liquid then cut leaves into 1 cm squares.

Dressing

Mix ingredients together. Pour over the salad and allow to marinate for 20 minutes before serving.

Composition

Garnish the salad with sesame seeds and sprigs of coriander.

Cucumber and bitter green salad with lime dressing

A Thai-style dressing with a Mediterranean-style salad makes this another cross-cultural experience that works surprisingly well. Ground shrimp is the basis for many Thai-style dishes, especially salads. You may find its aroma overpowering, but once combined with other ingredients it becomes quite subtle.

Cucumber and bitter green salad

2 continental cucumbers
1 red onion
1 bunch fresh mint

1 bunch fresh watercress
1 bunch fresh coriander
60 g rocket, washed

Lime dressing

1 clove garlic
juice of 3 fresh limes
1 teaspoon ground dried shrimp
2 red chillies, seeded and chopped

2 teaspoons fish sauce
1 tablespoon stock syrup
(see page 232)

Cucumber and bitter green salad

Peel cucumbers and cut into large, round slices. Cut the onion in half and again into thin slices. Wash and separate the bunches of mint, watercress and coriander into sprigs and combine with the rocket.

Dressing

Combine ingredients thoroughly.

Composition

Combine cucumber, bitter greens, onion and dressing in a large mixing bowl, tossing lightly to mix, and serve immediately.

Deep-fried mussels in soft batter

This is a simple dish but it is one of my favourite ways of cooking mussels and ideal for a very informal occasion.

Batter

2 egg yolks	125 g plain flour
250 ml iced water	125 g cornflour
½ teaspoon salt	2 eggwhites
½ teaspoon sugar	
½ teaspoon freshly ground	
black pepper	

Mussels

1 kg black mussels, cleaned	olive oil
and bearded	

Garnish

chilli sauce or lemon wedges

Batter

Whisk egg yolks and iced water together, then add salt, sugar and pepper. Sift flour and cornflour together. Slowly add the liquid to the flour and mix until it is a smooth paste. (I prefer to use my hand to squeeze out the lumps to avoid creating more gluten in the flour.)

Whisk eggwhites until stiff and fold into the batter.

Mussels

Steam or cook the mussels in boiling water for just 3 minutes. The shells should be just open. Using a teaspoon, scoop the mussels out of the shells. Any unopened mussels should be discarded (these are stale).

Strain off the liquid and dip mussels in the batter. Deep-fry in the olive oil until golden.

Composition

Serve with chilli sauce for dipping or a lemon wedge.

Kangaroo Moroccan style with couscous and chick peas

A teaching colleague wanted to do a Moroccan-style lamb dish, marinated with cumin, fenugreek, mint, coriander, yoghurt, saffron, lemon and garlic, then baked. I suggested using kangaroo instead of lamb and chargrilling the meat instead of baking it. It turned out to be superb. Kangaroo does not have a strong game flavour and it needs to be boosted. Excellent quality meat is available, but if it is not done properly it can have a slightly rank flavour; the Moroccan marinade is the answer to that. We experimented by boiling up some of the marinade, adding kangaroo-tail brown stock and using the combination as a sauce to moisten the dish. It worked. I put it on the menu at The Running Man restaurant in Adelaide when I was consulting there in 1991 and it received a rave reaction.

This is a Moroccan tandoori dish with some licence in the interpretation. Developed by Cheong at Regency Hotel School, it has since hopped onto many hotel and restaurant menus. It is incredibly fragrant and must be accompanied by perfectly cooked couscous and chickpeas to be a total success. It could be called very Australian as it exudes the sense of adventure that we enjoy in this country. Pay special attention to the grilling technique, which can make or break the dish.

12 kangaroo fillets

Marinade
1.2 litres yoghurt
*1 tablespoon ground
  coriander seeds*
2½ tablespoons cumin powder
4 tablespoons fenugreek powder
1 teaspoon saffron
*2 whole garlic bulbs, cut in half
  horizontally*
1 tablespoon chopped parsley

½ cup olive oil
1 teaspoon salt
juice and skin of 4 lemons
5 whole fresh chillies
¼ bunch mint
1 bunch coriander roots
2 tablespoons lentil flour
2 tablespoons extra yoghurt

Couscous and chick peas

50 g chickpeas, skins removed
250 g couscous
2 tablespoons olive oil
5 whole shallots, finely chopped
2 cloves garlic, finely chopped
2 tomatoes, skinned, seeded
  and cubed

zest of 1 lemon, cut into fine
  strips and blanched
2 tablespoons finely chopped
  Italian parsley
mint, cut into fine strips

Marinade

Mix all marinade ingredients (except lentil flour and the extra yoghurt) together and add kangaroo fillets. Marinate for 12 hours. Reserve the marinade for use during grilling.

Couscous and chickpeas

Boil the chickpeas until they are tender. Prepare the couscous by placing it on a muslin cloth in a steamer and steaming for 25 minutes. By then it should be soft and fluffy.

In a frying-pan heat up the olive oil and add shallots, garlic, tomatoes and lemon zest. Mix in the couscous and chickpeas then the parsley and mint.

When ready to cook the kangaroo, make sure that the grill is clean and hot before you start. Grill kangaroo fillets until medium rare, paying constant attention to ensure that the flame is neither too low nor too high.

To make a sauce, strain the lemon zest off the marinade and bring the remaining liquid to the boil. Thicken with lentil flour mixed with the extra yoghurt.

Composition

 Slice the meat and serve on a bed of couscous and chickpeas. Spoon the cooked marinade generously over the meat and around the couscous.

White pork slices with garlic sauce

This is a simple and delicious dish for pork lovers. The belly pork in this recipe is streaked with fat, but boiling reduces the fat considerably. If belly pork is too fatty for your liking, you can use shoulder pork; ask the butcher to roll it first. The meat should have a slight crunch to it—a little surprise for a boiled meat dish—and be very thinly sliced. The garlic sauce is pungent and tasty and typically Asian in style.

Pork
500 g belly pork
1 tablespoon salt

1 large slice ginger
2 spring onions

Garlic sauce
2 tablespoons chopped garlic
2½ tablespoons sweet dark
  soy sauce

1 tablespoon white chicken
  stock (see page 224)
1 teaspoon chilli oil

Cut the skin away from the pork. Bring 2 litres of water to the boil. Blanch the pork in the boiling water then refresh in cold water. Change the water, bring to the boil, add salt, ginger and spring onions. Add the pork again and remove any scum that floats to the top. Turn flame to a simmer and cook for 30 minutes.

Remove pork from the water and insert a skewer into the meat. Check the fluid that runs out—it should be clear without any trace of blood. When the pork is done, remove it from the pot and allow to stand for 30 minutes. Slice it into very thin slices and arrange on a serving plate. Bring the stock back to the boil and ladle over the pork slices. (The last step ensures that the pork is completely cooked. If the meat is still pink after one ladle of stock, repeat the process.) Drain the stock off the plate before serving.

For garlic sauce, mix the ingredients together thoroughly.

Composition

 Pour the sauce over the pork slices. Garnish with fresh coriander.

Chinese shortcake served with jasmine tea

This is a sweet dish traditionally served with jasmine tea at the close of a Chinese banquet. The tea assists the digestion and refreshes the palate. The shortcake is simple to prepare and inexpensive. Tik Kuan Yin tea from the Fujian region is a particularly good variety to serve with this sweet.

200 g lard
160 g sugar
1 large egg, room temperature
320 g flour
½ tablespoon double-action
  baking powder

2 tablespoons custard powder
1 teaspoon bicarb soda
320 g lotus seed paste
1 egg yolk, lightly beaten

Preheat the oven to 190°C. Using either a wooden spoon or your fingers, cream the lard, sugar and egg until light and fluffy. Sift flour, baking powder, custard powder and bicarb soda together. Mix ingredients by pressing into the palm of the hand. Try to avoid kneading too much.

Roll the dough into a 4 cm thick log. Divide into 4 cm long pieces and place on a cool working surface. Dust the lotus seed paste with a little flour and roll into a 2 cm thick log and divide into 4 cm long pieces. Place the dough and paste pieces alternately in a line to check that the dough is exactly double the thickness of the paste. If not quite double, add or take away as much dough or paste as necessary. Then roll each piece of dough into a ball and flatten in the palm of the hand. Place a piece of lotus seed paste in the centre of the dough. Gather the edge of the dough together to form a ball, enclosing the paste completely. Flatten slightly until about 3 cm in height.

Place on baking paper and bake for 20 minutes. Brush with egg yolk wash and return to the oven for a short time until glazed.

Liew Family Gathering

The Liew 'family' in South Australia is smaller than the one we knew as children in Kuala Lumpur, Malaysia, where five families lived on one farm. There are nine children of my generation in my family, so by Australian standards our gatherings are quite large. Typically, you will see my mum and dad and parents-in-law in one group, then all their children and one or two of our cousins, a few close friends and any visiting relatives in a second, and all our children in a third. When the celebratory table is covered with wonderfully aromatic dishes, simply prepared and so inviting, we are like three overlapping circles that form one. Around 50 or so come to eat, commune and renew the ties.

Renewing the ties is important when one has come to a new country. I am sure this is how my great grandparents and my grandparents must have felt when they went to Malaysia from China. Family gatherings made everyone feel more secure. It is easy to forget that like us, they were migrants too. It seems like we are always moving, and always having Liew family gatherings. Some of us came to Australia over twenty years ago; others arrived later, after a separation of ten years. We have different skills—our fields cover medicine, early Australian furniture, nursing, law, landscape gardening and, of course, cooking. My father has even been acting in films since he came here. Some have gone to live in Canada, Brazil, and Saudi Arabia; we are very successful at adapting. In Australia we value the peace, stability, educational opportunities and tolerance that this country offers. Perhaps these seem commonplace, but if you have ever experienced different circumstances, you might not take them for granted. We do not.

The food at our gatherings is both an expression of our past and of our adaptation to a new society. As we begin to understand our new place and culture, the food begins to reflect that. We did the same on the farm in Malaysia when we started to cook curry. At Christmas, now, my sister Kwei-Lan stuffs turkey with fruits and Chinese sticky rice and uses a curry sauce to braise it—the combination speaks for itself.

You will find a marvellous density of flavour in this menu. Many of them are our 'miss most' dishes, the ones we used to buy from the abundant hawker stalls in Malaysia, but which we had to make for ourselves when we migrated. These dishes are designed to be served buffet style reflecting a sense of sharing and family informality. If you wish to try them individually you may need to prepare rice or noodles as an accompaniment. A buffet allows everyone to try a large selection of dishes and while there may be rice or noodles on the table, they are not the mainstay.

The exception would be the nonya curry. It is difficult for anyone from South-East Asia, or for admirers of South-East Asian dishes, to contemplate a curry without rice. However, if you are caught with no rice in the cupboard, try the overseas student trick of eating it with white bread. It is still delicious!

Liew Family Gathering recipes

INDIAN ROJAK

DINGWU VEGETARIAN PLATTER

LOQUAT MANDOLIN-SHAPED DUCK

NONYA-STYLE KORMA CHICKEN CURRY

BLACK BEAN AND CHILLI RICE VERMICELLI

MONGOLIAN-STYLE DEEP-FRIED SPICED GOAT

GRANDMA'S FUN KWOR

THAI-STYLE BAKED MULLOWAY

RED-ROAST CHICKEN SALAD
WITH A CHILLI-OIL VINAIGRETTE

STIR-FRIED SOUTHERN KING PRAWNS
WITH ASPARAGUS AND ABALONE MUSHROOMS

STEAMED EGGPLANT WITH TOMATO CHILLI SAUCE

FRESH FRUIT TAPIOCA PUDDING WITH PALM SUGAR

Indian rojak

I remember the Indian rojak man. At around half past three in the afternoon he arrives carrying two large baskets, with two tiers in each basket, both suspended from a pole. One basket contains all the necessary condiments to make the rojak and the other is filled with all the tempting nonya keuh or sweet and savoury snacks. Having finished lunch at two, my father enjoys a nibble at this time of the day. The child who is helping to mind the shop with him is the lucky one—he or she will usually be offered a serve of the rojak. Some of my brothers and sisters are satisfied with the nonya keuh but my choice is the rojak because it is hot and spicy. Watching the rojak man I see him bring out one little stool to sit on and another to serve as his chopping board. He then puts together the salad, chopping all the ingredients at great speed, with an accurate and typically Asian preparatory rhythm.

Rojak is a kind of vegetarian salad, except for the seafood! It has chilli, calamari and wadai—an Indian 'felafel' made with chana dahl (yellow chickpeas)—bean curd, coconut fingers, battered prawns, blanched bean sprouts, shredded cucumber and lettuce smothered in a sesame and sweet-potato sauce. Another element is spicy coconut calamari, which is prepared with a 'rempah' base—a mix of herbs, spices and vegetables ground into a paste for curries and other spiced dishes. There are many varieties. Allow plenty of time for this dish as each component must be

prepared separately. Read the recipe through first to familiarise yourself
with the steps, then read it once more.

Rojak

100 g desirée potatoes,
  boiled in their jackets and
  cut into batons
6 wadai (see below)
6 coconut fingers (see below)
3 deep-fried bean curd cakes,
  sliced

6 prawn fritters (see below)
300 g bean sprouts, blanched
1 cucumber, shredded
2 lettuce leaves (cos or iceberg),
  shredded
spicy coconut calamari (see below)

Garnish

2 hard-boiled eggs, cut into quarters   sprigs of fresh coriander

Sauce

1 tablespoon salt
100 g tamarind
250 g orange sweet potato
2½ tablespoons white vinegar
300 g sugar
2½ tablespoons chopped onion
1 clove garlic, finely chopped

5 dried chillies, seeded
1 teaspoon blachan
100 ml peanut oil
2 tablespoons toasted
  sesame seeds, finely ground
2 tablespoons toasted
  sesame seeds

Add the salt to 600 ml water and soak the tamarind for about 10 minutes
until the seeds can be squeezed out of the fruit. Strain and reserve the
water, then purée the tamarind flesh. Boil and mash the sweet potato then
force through a sieve.

Add vinegar and sugar to tamarind water and set aside. Blend onion,
garlic, dried chillies and blachan paste into a fine paste. Heat the oil in a
saucepan, add the paste and fry until it is fragrant and the oil separates.
Add in tamarind liquid and sweet potato mash. Bring this mixture to the
boil and add ground sesame seeds and whole sesame seeds and simmer
gently for 30 minutes until it thickens.

Coconut fingers

20 g dried shrimp
120 g plain flour
½ teaspoon salt
½ teaspoon freshly ground black
  pepper

1 teaspoon sugar
120 g fresh grated coconut (or
  desiccated coconut)
1½ tablespoons chickpea flour
oil

Soak the dried shrimp in plenty of water to soften it, then grind finely. In a bowl, mix ground shrimp with flour, salt, pepper and sugar. Add coconut, chickpea flour and half a cup of water and mix into a dough. Shape dough into six 2 cm x 6 cm logs and deep-fry at a moderate temperature until golden brown.

Wadai

200 g chana dahl (chick peas)
  soaked overnight, water
  changed 2 or 3 times
1 large onion, finely chopped
1 fresh chilli, finely chopped
½ teaspoon cumin seeds
½ teaspoon finely chopped
  fresh coriander

¼ teaspoon bicarb soda
100 g plain flour
½ teaspoon salt
1 teaspoon sugar
oil for deep-frying
2½ tablespoons water

Blend soaked chana dahl into a fine paste. Add onion, chilli, cumin seeds and coriander. Sift bicarb soda with the flour and add to the paste with the salt, sugar and water. Work into a soft dough and set aside 100 g of wadai dough for the prawn fritters. Heat the oil and, using a tablespoon, separate the remaining dough into 6 pieces and deep-fry on moderate heat until wadai float to the top. Set wadai aside on kitchen paper.

If you have enough dough to make more than 6 wadai, cook this too and present as a snack.

Prawn fritters

6 large prawns (see preparing
  prawns page 220)
100 g wadai dough (reserved above)
2½ tablespoons self-raising flour

salt
½ teaspoon English mustard powder
peanut oil
3 tablespoons water

Butterfly the prawns by cutting down the backs and flattening out the meat. Mix wadai mixture with self-raising flour, salt, mustard powder and water to make a batter. Dip the prawns in the batter and fry in hot oil until golden brown. Set aside on kitchen paper.

Spicy coconut calamari

2 teaspoons chilli powder
6 candlenuts
2 tablespoons finely chopped
  shallots
1 teaspoon blachan
½ teaspoon freshly ground
  black pepper

½ cup peanut oil
500 g calamari, cleaned and gutted
  (whole, plus severed tentacles)
120 g coconut cream
½ teaspoon cumin seeds,
  finely ground into powder
2 teaspoons sugar

Grind the chilli powder, candlenuts, shallots, blachan and pepper into a curry paste known as 'rempah'.

Heat the oil and fry the ground paste until it is fragrant and the oil has separated. Add whole calamari, tentacles and coconut cream and simmer gently until the sauce thickens. Add cumin powder and sugar. The calamari should be cooked gently until tender and moist, stirring regularly to prevent sticking. Remove cooked whole calamari from the sauce and cut into rings half a centimetre in width. Return to sauce.

Composition

Put potato batons on the base of the plate. Cut wadai and coconut fingers into bite-size pieces and place on top of the batons. Slice bean curd and prawn fritters and place on top next, followed by bean sprouts, shredded cucumber and lettuce. Pour the sauce over the salad. Spoon spicy calamari over the top and garnish with hard-boiled egg quarters and sprigs of fresh coriander.

Dingwu vegetarian platter

This is the speciality of my mother, Cheong Sow Keng. She travelled to Dingwu mountain in Guanzhou, China, an area renowned for its vegetarian dishes, and has prepared this particular dish ever since. Knowing that the younger generation is not prepared to devote the necessary hours to its creation at this stage of their lives she usually serves it at Liew family gatherings. Being the chef of the family I have often prepared this dish (always with her guidance) for Chinese New Year or Moon Festival dinners at Neddy's. The dish includes many dried ingredients which offer a lesson on the Chinese way in themselves. Imagine the various special dried foods, such as oysters, black moss, and cloud-ear fungus, carefully suspended from their high ceilings, safe in the dry atmosphere for a family celebration worthy of their revival. These 'treasure' foods were also bought as gifts, always at the ready. Learning to cook this dish made me realise how very practical and precise the Chinese approach to food and life is; the surprise is that the result is so sophisticated.

Like the recipe for Indian Rojak, this dish has a number of separate ingredients which must be individually prepared before they are combined to create the final dish. For this reason, start by examining each element of the recipe, and prepare for a lengthy visit to the local Chinese grocery. You won't have difficulty finding anything—they are all standard Chinese ingredients. Some groceries offer packaged Dingwu treasure foods, but it's far more entertaining to seek out the individual packets and make new discoveries along each aisle. There is no vegetable or animal the Chinese have not managed to transform into something edible!

Vegetables

20 g black moss
18 fried gluten balls
120 g dried bean curd sticks
6 pieces Chinese cabbage,
   white stem part only
peanut oil
6 whole ginkgo nuts
   (or tinned variety)
200 g winter bamboo shoot
40 g lily buds
20 g cloud-ear fungus
18 whole Chinese black
   mushrooms

pinch of salt
1 tablespoon ginger juice
1 tablespoon spring onion juice
1 tablespoon light soy sauce
1 tablespoon sesame oil
1 tablespoon cornflour
6 whole red dates
12 large whole dried oysters
   (omit if strictly vegetarian)
1 spring onion, white only
1 cm knob ginger, slightly crushed
6 slices lotus root

Seasoning

2 tablespoons peanut oil
1 tablespoon finely chopped garlic
1 tablespoon finely chopped ginger
1 finely chopped spring onion,
   white only
1 tablespoon rice wine

1 tablespoon brown bean paste
1 teaspoon fermented red
   bean curd
1 teaspoon fermented white
   bean curd
1 tablespoon sugar

Sauce

3 tablespoons hoi sin sauce
1 tablespoon light soy sauce
2 tablespoons oyster sauce

1 teaspoon wheat starch
1 teaspoon English mustard powder
1 teaspoon white vinegar

Vegetables

Black moss: Bring to the boil with some water then rinse in cold water to remove dust and grit. Add to oysters during final simmering period, as below.

Fried gluten balls: Soak in hot water until soft.

Dried bean curd sticks: Deep-fry until the oil bubbles and is golden. Remove the sticks and soak them in hot water to remove the fat. Cut the sticks into 6 cm pieces then cook gently in a clean pot of water until limp.

Chinese cabbage: Lightly fry in oil on medium heat for no more than a few seconds. Cut into strips.

Ginkgo nuts: Crack the shells, blanch the nuts in hot water and remove the skins. (The tinned variety are already cleaned and prepared.)

Winter bamboo: Slice into 1 cm thick pieces and deep-fry until golden.

Lily buds: Soak in warm water until soft. Cut the hard end off the stem and tie the lily bud in a knot.

Cloud-ear fungus: Wash thoroughly and pat dry. Dry toast in a wok over moderate heat. It needs very little cooking (not much more than 1 minute), and is then ready to be added to the dish.

Chinese black mushrooms: Remove stems and put mushroom caps in a saucepan covered with water and bring to the boil. Discard the liquid and wash the mushrooms thoroughly. Return mushrooms to saucepan and cover with water. Make a marinade with salt, ginger and spring onion juice, soy sauce, sesame oil and cornflour and marinate the mushrooms for 10 minutes.

Red dates: Soak in warm water until reconstituted and remove seeds.

Dried oysters: Soak the dried oysters in 2 cups of water for 2 hours. Bring the water to the boil, remove the oysters and retain the liquid. Remove any shell or grit from the oysters then return them to the liquid, add spring onion and ginger and simmer for 30 minutes or until tender. Add black moss for the last 15 minutes of the simmering period (see above).

Seasoning

Heat the oil in a large pot and fry the garlic, ginger and spring onion until fragrant, then douse with rice wine. Add brown bean paste, red and white fermented bean curd and fry until glossy.

Add the sugar, fried gluten balls, bean curd stick, ginkgo nuts, winter bamboo, lily buds, Chinese black mushrooms, red dates and lotus root and fry together for a few minutes. Add water to just cover the ingredients and simmer for 45 minutes. Mix in cloud-ear fungus for the last 5 minutes of cooking time. Reserve the liquid for use in the sauce.

Using a 22–25 cm medium depth bowl (a Pyrex baking-dish depth), layer

the ingredients: place the Chinese mushroom at the very bottom, then some bean-curd sticks, then oysters, black moss, ginkgo nuts, lily buds, cloud-ear fungus, fried gluten balls, lotus roots and red dates, then more bean-curd sticks covered with Chinese cabbage stems.

Sauce

Mix some of the cooking liquid reserved above (about 300 ml) with hoi sin sauce, soy sauce and oyster sauce and fill up the bowl containing the vegetables. Cover the bowl with a plate or plastic wrap. Steam in a steamer for 45 minutes. Set remaining liquid aside in a saucepan. Remove the bowl from the steamer and take off the covering. Taking a clean, cold plate, angle the bowl to drain the liquid from the vegetables into the saucepan and thicken with wheat starch. Mix together the mustard and vinegar and add to the liquid. This sauce can be adjusted with sugar or more hoi sin to taste.

Composition

 Slide the vegetables onto a serving platter large enough to hold the 'mould' of vegetables. Spoon over the sauce.

Loquat mandolin-shaped duck

*I first created this dish at Coriole Winery in McLaren Vale, for a wine
and food event in the mid-1980s. I used a 44-gallon drum to roast the
ducks and four specially-made roasting forks for skewering them.
Liz, John, Mary, our children and I slept there the night before in read-
iness for the onslaught the next day. We used olive-tree wood on the fire
and the ducks were so crisp and fragrant that we sold out. We even sold
the necks. Tim Pak Poy—now owner of Claude's in Sydney—helped me
with the roasting, the remainder of our party with the service.*

None of us will forget the setting at Coriole—emerald lawn fringed by white
daisies overlooking vineyards turning red and yellow in autumn. They also
make green-gold olive oil at Coriole now—another reason to rejoice in the
Adelaide environs. The garnish of young vine leaves is in honour of Coriole.

The title of this dish is a direct translation from the Chinese. The ducks are
split open along the back to create the shape and to tighten the skin for
crispness. They are further tightened with hot acidulated water, marinated,
dried for twelve hours, and then roasted in the oven. The marinade per-
meates through to the bone and the skin is biscuity, smoky, and crisp. To
the Chinese the skin is the most important part of this dish and the chef
will be judged accordingly. To achieve the desired result, don't
skimp on the drying process before roasting. If you want to be really
adventurous, try spit-roasting the bird (or birds) over fruit-wood embers,
slowly, skin-side first. The scent of the fruit wood will permeate the duck.

Duck-skin glaze

3 tablespoons maltose
6 tablespoons vinegar

3 tablespoons water

Mandolin duck

1.8 kg duck
1 tablespoon prickly ash
2 slices lemon
1 teaspoon garlic, finely chopped
1 teaspoon ginger, finely chopped
1 teaspoon finely chopped
  spring onion, white only

1 teaspoon brown bean paste
1 tablespoon hoi sin sauce
1 teaspoon chopped
  coriander roots
2 teaspoons Chinese rose wine

Duck-skin glaze

Mix ingredients together. Set aside.

Mandolin duck

Split duck open along the spine and flatten it. Season the inside of the duck with prickly ash. Take two pieces of wood about 4 cm wide x 1 cm thick and force one to sit across the breast bone between the two wings and the second between the two legs, taking care not to damage the skin.

Heat a pot of water and add lemon slices. As it comes to the boil, ladle the water over the skin side of the duck and watch the skin tighten. Mix together the garlic, ginger, spring onion, brown bean paste, hoi sin sauce, coriander roots and Chinese rose wine and brush some over the flesh and bone side of the duck. Brush the skin with the glaze then hang the duck in a cool place to dry for about 12 hours. If you have a fan, place the duck in front of the air stream and reduce the drying time by 6 hours.

Preheat the oven to 220°C. Place the duck on the rack and put a drip tray containing 1 cup of water underneath it to collect the drips of fat. Roast for 20 minutes then turn down the heat to 180°C and cook for a further 30 minutes. The duck skin—the most prized part—should be crispy and mahogany-coloured. Remove wood and chop the duck into large pieces.

Composition

 Arrange young vine leaves (if in season) over a platter and place the duck pieces on top.

Nonya-style korma chicken curry

I remember the old lady who comes to my father's shop in the evening, to visit and to sell curry to my grandmother. She carries a basket up the stairs with her containing a little warmer, and on top, a nonya curry. The two large bowls are yellow-red-orange in colour with a thin layer of oil on top and a rich presence of coconut milk. She uses a good quality chicken just cooked, not dry but succulent. They tell me that this lady makes only this dish.

This is a very common Chinese version of chicken curry. My maternal aunt was the expert on nonya cooking in our family through her own family associations and having been a governess for one of the sons of the Sultan of Selangor. She used to invite us to her house and teach my mother her nonya style dishes—the most memorable being a crocodile curry with pineapple. My aunt would use the authentic slow frying technique, stirring diligently until the moisture from the coconut milk has evaporated and the oil begins to separate out. Her patience was the essence of her success.

Nonya cuisine derives from the blending of Chinese and Malay cooking knowledge, through trade and migration. In Malacca, the Portuguese influence adds another layer. Nonyas have a mixed background therefore, but their cultural identity is mainly Chinese. Nonya refers to the females; babas to the males.

Nonya cooking knowledge was traditionally passed on from mother to daughter and the secrets were carefully guarded. Overseas demand has created an interest in this style throughout Asia, leading to the publication of a few cookbooks on nonya technique and dishes. The secret of this dish is fresh coconut milk. Ask your Chinese grocer to prepare freshly grated coconut, put it in a muslin bag and squeeze out the first cream—the richest and creamiest. The second squeezing produces a thinner milkier liquid with plenty of flavour. This second milk is the one used during the cooking of the nonya curry. Just before serving add the first cream to introduce a creamy richness. If using tinned coconut milk, use the cream around the edge of the tin as the first cream. The fennel gives extra fragrance.

Rempah

1½ tablespoons roasted
  coriander seeds
½ teaspoon cumin seeds
½ teaspoon white pepper
4 cloves garlic

8 whole candlenuts
2 stalks lemon grass
10 coriander roots
½ tablespoon fennel seeds

Korma chicken

1.2 kg chicken
3 tablespoons peanut oil
2 teaspoons salt
2 cloves garlic, finely chopped
150 g shallots, finely chopped
1 cinnamon stick
1½ tablespoons finely chopped
  ginger

3 dried whole chillies, seeded
2 cardamom pods
300 ml coconut milk
2 tablespoons coconut cream
  (from the rim of the tin)

Garnish

fresh coriander leaves
shredded cucumber

sliced fresh red chillies
deep-fried shallots

Rempah

Using a vitamiser or mortar and pestle, blend the rempah ingredients into a very fine, smooth paste, adding a little water if necessary.

Korma chicken

Cut chicken into walnut-sized pieces.

In a pot, heat the oil and add the salt, garlic, shallots, cinnamon stick, ginger, chillies and cardamom pods and fry until fragrant.

Add rempah and fry until the oil separates. Add the coconut cream at this point to help slow down the heat and avoid burning the spices and ruining the flavour. Do not rush this step.

Add chicken pieces, stir and cook for 3 minutes. Add coconut milk and simmer for 30 minutes or until chicken is tender.

Composition

Place the curry into a shallow bowl and garnish with coriander, cucumber, sliced chillies and deep-fried shallots. Serve with steamed white rice.

Black bean and chilli rice vermicelli

This is the first dish I learnt to cook in my father's restaurant—for the staff, not the customers. I was about fourteen and the chef who was cooking for the customers gave me instructions on the side. It is a personal favourite because it is hot, fragrant, and served with plenty of sauce—a regular at our family gatherings.

Rice vermicelli, the thinnest of noodles, are an appetising choice for a snack or luncheon dish. They are easy to prepare, but be careful not to overcook them—soaking 'cooks' them in any case. Prepare each element beforehand—a necessary discipline for Chinese noodle dishes like this one. While you could omit the chilli, the flavour will not be so intense and complex. Try halving the amount if you are feeling tentative. The garnish of spring onion gives a fresh flavour and a burst of colour.

Rice vermicelli

3 teaspoons dried black beans
425 g rice vermicelli
140 ml peanut oil
1 dried chilli
3 fresh red chillies
3 cloves garlic, finely chopped
2 cm knob ginger, shredded
100 g chicken fillet, cut into very
   thin strips

100 g lean pork, cut into very
   thin strips
120 g green prawns, cut into
   very thin strips (see page 220)
½ green capsicum, finely
   shredded

1 tablespoon oyster sauce
3 teaspoons dark soy sauce
1 teaspoon white pepper
150 ml brown chicken stock

1½ tablespoon cornflour
2 teaspoons sesame oil
2 teaspoons salt
2 tablespoons sugar

Garnish

2 spring onions, finely chopped
shredded Chinese lettuce

fresh coriander leaves

Rice vermicelli

Soak the black beans in ⅓ of a cup of warm water for a few minutes, then drain. This softens them and reduces their saltiness. Soak the rice vermicelli in warm water until it swells and turns white and soft. Strain into a colander and shake the noodles until no more water drips out. This ensures that there will be no dangerous splatters when frying the noodles.

In a wok, heat about 100 ml of the oil and oil the surface of the wok well. Put in the rice vermicelli and spread over the wok to an even thickness. Fry gently but do not brown too much. Avoid stirring vermicelli; instead, use a wok chan or fish lifter and occasionally lift the bottom of the vermicelli so that it does not stick to the wok. Then turn the noodles over and repeat on the other side, adding a little more oil if necessary. Lift the rice vermicelli cake onto a Chinese spider (a flat, long-handled strainer) and strain off excess oil, shaking it a few times, then set aside.

Heat the remaining oil in the wok and fry dried and fresh chilli, black beans, garlic, and ginger for a few seconds over medium heat. Add chicken, pork, prawns and green capsicum and fry, loosening the chicken threads so they separate (they have a tendency to stick).

Seasoning mix thickener

Combine the seasoning mix thickener ingredients, add to the wok and bring to the boil. Add in the rice vermicelli and combine until the mixture is even and the sauce is thick enough to coat the noodles.

Composition

 Serve noodles on a platter garnished with spring onions, Chinese lettuce and coriander.

Mongolian-style deep-fried spiced goat

This is a northern Chinese style of dish. I've given it a southern touch. It might look dark and primitive, but I can assure you it is an exciting dish; the aromatic fragrances of the spices and rich flavour of the goat is very appetising, and when you put it in your mouth, it's so light to eat.

This recipe demands a combination of simmering and frying—a 'double technique' often used in the preparation of Chinese pork dishes. The ginger and spring onion in the stock cut the raw rank flavour of the simmering goat and are also used for chicken and pork. The double cooking of the goat means that one does not have to be experienced in choosing the best meat. The shoulder or neck has a strong, dependable, hearty peasant flavour. Leave sufficient time for the goat to be completely cooked in the stock before being cubed and fried.

Seasoning mixture
2 spring onions
2 tablespoons sliced ginger
2 whole star anise
2 teaspoons licorice roots
2 pieces tangerine peel, dried
½ teaspoon Sichuan peppercorns

600 ml superior light soy sauce
250 ml yellow rice wine
2 dried chillies
1 tablespoon salt

Goat
1 slice fresh ginger
1 spring onion
1 kg shoulder or neck of goat,
  boned
2½ tablespoons rock sugar
cornflour for dusting

1 litre peanut oil
10 g prickly ash
1 cos lettuce
2 bunches white asparagus,
  steamed
1 teaspoon rendered chicken fat

Seasoning mixture
Put seasoning mixture ingredients in a pot with 1.5 litres of water and bring to the boil. Simmer slowly for 20 minutes.

Goat

Bring to the boil a large pot of water (deep enough to submerge the meat), and add the ginger and spring onion. Blanch the shoulder or neck of goat in the boiling water for 15 minutes, remove it, rinse and drain.

Plunge the goat in the seasoning mixture and bring to the boil, removing any impurities floating on the top, then simmer slowly for 1 hour. Add rock sugar in the last 15 minutes.

Cool the meat in the liquid until cold.

Cut goat into 4 x 4 cm cubes and dust with cornflour. Heat the oil in a wok over a moderate heat, deep-fry goat pieces a few at a time for 2 minutes and remove. Heat oil again until it starts to smoke, deep-fry goat pieces again until crisp. Rest fried goat pieces on kitchen paper and sprinkle with prickly ash.

Composition

Using a generous serving platter, fan out cos lettuce leaves at one end of the platter and white asparagus spears at the other end. Moisten the spears with a little rendered chicken fat. Place goat cubes in the centre of the platter.

Grandma's fun kwor

Every Chinese village traditionally has its particular style of fun kwor depending on ingredients—meat or vegetables. I remember Grandmother making this style for her own birthday. She was the head chef and organiser of the family and she always had a brigade of several daughters and daughters-in-law as well as cousins, friends and neighbours to help out when the big preparation day came around. Her party was usually a very large affair, with up to a hundred guests. Grandmother and Grandfather were always very popular; they had been known for a long time in the community and relatives came from all around for the birthday celebrations. Many came from Kelumpang where my great-grandfather and family started their life in Malaysia after they left China.

Fun kwor are either shallow-fried in oil or steamed—my grandmother preferred them steamed. The women would sit in a circle and make the fun kwor, and the kids would also have a go with the scrap dough, but the aunties had the nimble fingers necessary for perfect packaging. It was wonderful to watch. Now both the women and the men of the family make them.

The principal requirement for this recipe is patience and skill in folding the pastry. If you have any opportunity to watch an experienced person making dim sum—the dumplings served for Chinese yum cha—then take it. Seeing how it's done will help. Fun kwor is the easiest dim sum recipe of the lot, so it is an excellent starting place for anyone who wishes to master the art of the delicate dim sum.

Filling

1 tablespoon cornflour
1 tablespoon water
1 tablespoon olive oil
80 g dried shrimp, roughly
  chopped
80 g pork fat, finely minced
240 g pork fillet, finely minced
160 g Chinese salted turnip,
  finely chopped

160 g water chestnuts, diced
1 bunch garlic chives,
  finely chopped
40 g roasted peanuts,
  roughly chopped
1 chilli, finely minced
1 tablespoon rice wine
½ tablespoon salt
1 tablespoon sugar

Pastry

pinch of salt
375 g wheat starch
80 g tapioca starch

400 ml water
1 tablespoon lard, melted

Filling

Mix the cornflour with 1 tablespoon of water. Heat the oil and sauté the dried shrimp, then add the pork fat, pork fillet, Chinese salted turnip, water chestnuts, garlic chives and peanuts and fry until the mixture is fairly dry but glazed. Add the chilli, rice wine, salt and sugar and thicken with the cornflour mixture. The filling should be slightly on the sweet side.

Pastry

Add the salt to the wheat starch and tapioca starch. Boil the water and stir in the starch mix to form a dough. Knead until even, taking care not to knead too much. Incorporate the lard into the dough and knead a little longer.

Roll pastry to 3 cm thick by 20 cm long and then divide into cubes. Roll each cube into a ball and flatten and roll out the pastry into a 6 cm diameter round. Place the filling mixture in the centre and seal the edges by folding over like a 'pasty'. Pinch the edges together until they equal the original thickness of the pastry. Steam the dumplings in a Chinese steamer or large covered plate over boiling water for 10 minutes.

Composition

Serve piping hot on a large plate.

Thai-style baked mulloway

We had decided to have a barbecue at my dad's place and a visiting friend (who spends most of his time travelling and whose main pastime is eating) told me about this dish. I managed to research it beforehand, finding one similar recipe in a Thai cookbook. Thai people normally use fillets—I decided to take advantage of Australia's large and tasty whole mulloway as a variation. That way it could easily serve up to ten people for an Australian backyard feast.

This dish has a special fragrance because it is baked in banana leaves. Unwrapped, the aromas of spice and coconut mingle with the subtle and essential fragrance of the dried shrimp and blachan. Do not be deterred by the pungent odour of the shrimp and blachan before you cook it. These essential Thai tastes work surprisingly well with an Australian mulloway barbecue.

Thai paste

½ cup dried shrimp
3 cm knob fresh laos root, grated
1 stalk lemon grass, chopped
2 shallots, chopped
3 cloves garlic
1 tablespoon palm sugar
(or white sugar)

3 tablespoons fish sauce
1½ tablespoons blachan paste
1 tablespoon chopped
coriander roots
1 teaspoon shredded lime zest
100 g desiccated coconut
125 ml coconut milk

Mulloway

1 whole mulloway, approx.
1 kg in weight
100 ml peanut oil
large banana leaves
¼ bunch basil leaves

8 dried chillies, seeded and
shredded
1 teaspoon shredded Kaffir
lime leaves

Thai paste

Put dried shrimp, laos root, lemon grass, shallots, garlic, palm sugar, fish sauce, blachan paste, coriander roots, lime zest, desiccated coconut and coconut milk in a vitamiser ideally or food processor and mix to a very fine paste.

Mulloway

Preheat the oven to 180°C. Scale and clean the mulloway. Heat oil and brown the mulloway on both sides. Remove and place on a banana leaf large enough to wrap the mulloway completely.

Spread the paste over the mulloway and sprinkle with basil leaves, shredded chillies and lime leaves. Turn the fish over and repeat on the other side. Wrap the fish up completely in banana leaves and secure by wrapping in aluminium foil.

Bake in the oven or grill over charcoal for 25 minutes. Unwrap and eat straight from the banana leaf.

Red-roast chicken salad with a chilli-oil vinaigrette

This dish was discovered and recommended by my mother. I presented it on Mondays at Neddy's in the 1980s, our Chinese banquet night. For $14.80 you could have a seven course Chinese style dinner. It was a lucky dip—no choices. If you decided to be in it, your first experience would be a series of cold dishes. These were especially interesting— vegetables, fresh and in season, smooth 'drunken' chicken, slightly crunchy strips of jellyfish, duck-liver sausage, roast duck, village style boiled peanuts and so on. It was a refreshing beginning, rather like an antipasto but more flavoursome. The next item on the menu was usually a poultry dish. One of these was based on a dish from the Fanshan restaurant, which also inspired the shark lips dish. I remember that its Chinese name was supposed to have been that of an emperor's favourite concubine—something like 'Swan contemplating the moon'. There was steamed chicken on the base, prawn quenelles, sautéed celery and braised scallops in this dish. Another Chinese banquet number was a Muslim style steamed lamb breast with star anise. I first tried this in Beijing where they steam the breast of lamb until it melts in the mouth—Tungpo style. Later this red-roast chicken dish was also on the daily lunch menu at Neddy's. It was perfect for the business lunch brigade—tasty, available promptly, and an alto- gether different way to eat chicken.

The chicken is marinated with soy sauce then deep-fried. The mixture of deep-fried soy sauce and chilli oil gives it a really aromatic flavour, while the rice vinegar makes it clean and refreshing, not fatty. The taste sensation is of vinegar, ginger and shallots exuding from the chicken, and you may find it hot—the spices that marinate the chicken are the key. If you are thinking of substituting mixed chicken pieces for a whole chicken, don't do it! Frying the skin on the whole chicken guarantees the unique flavour; the dish would be very different if you were to use chicken pieces. On the other hand, chicken wings, which are encased in skin, would give a similar result to the whole chicken, and drum- sticks with intact skins would be a second alternative.

Red-roast chicken

1.2 kg chicken
1 spring onion, finely chopped
2 cm knob ginger, finely chopped
1 tablespoon rice wine

1 teaspoon salt
1 tablespoon soy sauce
1.2 litres peanut oil

Chilli-oil vinaigrette

2 spring onions, finely chopped
2 cm knob ginger, finely chopped
3 tablespoons superior light
  soy sauce
2 tablespoons white chicken stock
  (see page 224)

1 tablespoon sesame oil
½ tablespoon chilli oil
2 tablespoons rice vinegar
1½ tablespoons sugar

Garnish

1 continental cucumber, sliced

Red-roast chicken

Ensure the chicken cavity is thoroughly cleaned then score the legs.
Combine the spring onion, ginger, rice wine, salt and soy sauce and pour
over the chicken, allowing to stand for one hour. Heat the oil and deep-fry
the chicken until it is crisp and brown, for approximately 25 minutes. Set
aside in a warm place.

Chilli-oil vinaigrette

Combine the vinaigrette ingredients thoroughly.

Composition

 Cut the warm chicken into bite-size pieces and arrange on a plate
with the cucumber. Pour dressing over the chicken.

Stir-fried southern king prawns with asparagus and abalone mushrooms

When my parents first came here they were delighted with the quality and taste of our prawns and, in season, the asparagus is fresh and delicious. Its linear shoots mixed together with the attractively curled prawns and the oblong mushrooms make a great combination.

This makes an ideal luncheon dish. The textures and colours are complimentary too—tender green asparagus, soft beige mushroom and crisp pink prawns, reflecting a typically Chinese obsession with contrast in order to achieve harmony. Adding the rice wine to the prawns before they are coated in the eggwhite brings out the prawn flavour, which is then trapped inside the layer of eggwhite and cornflour.

Prawns
250 g medium southern
   king prawns
1 tablespoon water
1 tablespoon rice wine

1 eggwhite
½ teaspoon cornflour
1 tablespoon peanut oil

Seasoning mix
2½ tablespoons water
1 teaspoon cornflour
1 teaspoon sesame oil

½ teaspoon salt
1 teaspoon sugar
pinch of white pepper

Asparagus and mushrooms

350 g asparagus spears
160 ml peanut oil
1 dried chilli, seeded
2 cm knob ginger, finely sliced
2 cloves garlic, finely chopped
and mashed

2 spring onions, cut into
3 cm pieces
80 g small, fresh abalone
mushrooms, halved
1 tablespoon rice wine

Prawns

Prepare the prawns following the method on page 220.

Seasoning mix

Combine all ingredients.

Asparagus and mushrooms

Peel any hard skin off the asparagus spears and cut into 7–8 cm pieces.

In a wok, heat about three-quarters of the oil and stir-fry prawns until just pink. Strain off the oil and set aside.

Reheat the remaining oil in the wok and stir-fry the dried chilli. Add ginger, garlic and spring onion and cook until fragrant, then add asparagus, mushrooms and rice wine and stir-fry for a couple of minutes.

Add the cooked prawns and seasoning mixture to the wok. Stir quickly until the sauce thickens and add a little more oil if required to give shine.

Composition

 Place prawns, asparagus and mushrooms on a serving plate. A traditional Chinese shallow blue fish serving bowl is ideal for presenting this dish.

Steamed eggplant with tomato chilli sauce

*This is a simple dish which was served at least once a week in my
family. As a child I found it challenging to eat at first but it then
became a firm favourite—although most of my brothers and sisters
avoided it. I prepared the eggplant in the same style at Neddy's, in the
octopus salad dish, and it was very well received. The Chinese always
sprinkle spring onion with white pepper, believing it accentuates the
flavours of both ingredients.*

The striking feature of this dish is the creaminess of the steamed eggplant.
First it should be lightly salted to take away any bitterness, although this
rule applies mainly to eggplants that are not well watered (ideally they
should be watered four times a day). In Asia the long variety is used
because it has fewer seeds. Avoid large old eggplants—there will be too
many seeds—and always choose those that are dark skinned and glossy.

The sauce adds to the flavour, but if you or your guests do not like chilli,
you can leave it out. Another way of serving it is to steam the eggplant
until it is soft, then to drizzle hot shallot oil and soy sauce over it.

Steamed eggplant
2 eggplants   2 whole cloves garlic,
salt   finely chopped
peanut oil

 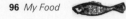

Tomato chilli sauce

1 tablespoon light soy sauce
1 tablespoon oyster sauce
3 tablespoons fresh tomato purée
(see page 221)

1 tablespoon sugar
½ tablespoon sesame oil
1 teaspoon chilli oil (optional)

Garnish

1 finely chopped spring onion,
white only

white pepper

Steamed eggplant

Cut eggplants lengthwise into 8 pieces. Lightly salt to remove bitterness; leave to stand for 10 minutes until beads of water appear on the surface, then dry with kitchen paper.

In a wok, heat up enough oil to shallow-fry. Add the garlic cloves and fry until light brown. Remove garlic and set aside. Brown each piece of egg-plant in the oil then remove and drain excess oil by placing on absorbent kitchen paper. Put the eggplant on a plate and put the browned garlic on top. Steam eggplant for 10 minutes in a Chinese steamer or a large covered plate over boiling water (don't forget to drain water off the plate).

Tomato chilli sauce

Mix together all ingredients.

Composition

 Pour sauce over the hot eggplant. Garnish with spring onion and sprinkle with white pepper. Serve at once.

Fresh fruit tapioca pudding with palm sugar

It looks like frog eggs, but don't be put off! This is a common hawker dish in Malaysia. Sago or tapioca is boiled up and served with fresh fruits. In Southern Australia, which has a temperate climate, we can use raspberries or kiwi fruit in place of tropical fruits if they are not available. We can also add the traditional mung beans to give it a nutty flavour. Condensed milk can be substituted for palm sugar, but the palm sugar is the best choice as it has flavour as well as sweetness. Westerners will be familiar with milk-based grain puddings, such as sago; this recipe offers an exciting variation.

250 g pearl sago
fresh fruits in season
160 g palm sugar (gula melaka)
1 heaped tablespoon treacle

2 paper-thin slices of ginger
1 pandan leaf
300 ml coconut milk

Soak sago in 1.5 litres of water for 30 minutes. Cut fruit into cubes or into balls, and leave berries whole.

Bring the sago and water to the boil and cook until soft. Strain off the water and wash off excess starch with cold water.

Meanwhile, make a syrup by bringing to the boil 400 ml water, palm sugar, treacle, ginger and pandan leaf until the sugar is dissolved. Strain and cool.

Combine one-third of the syrup with one-third of the coconut milk and mix into the sago. Place in cups or moulds and chill in the refrigerator for at least 1 hour.

Composition

 To serve, unmould the sago onto a plate of fresh fruit and pour over the remainder of the syrup and coconut milk.

Sunday Birthday Lunch Buffet

This collection reflects different times and experiences in my life and different stages of knowledge, all brought together. The menu is innovative, and leans towards a modern Australian style of dining—informal yet demanding, unpretentious yet sophisticated. To make these dishes I have had to spend time gaining an understanding of their cultural origins—either by reading and learning or absorbing knowledge from friends and acquaintances. This has allowed me to grasp the temperament of each dish.

Some say that learning how to do the dances or to prepare the food of a particular culture is a way of entering that culture—another language apart from language itself...I enjoy interpreting and expressing a particular culture through its food, but with my own signature and ideas to extend it. The result is generally fresh and exciting, and I love to do this type of cuisine when cooking for friends. I imagine it is a similar feeling to that of a dancer who hears their music. I identify my own approach with flamenco, with its traditional discipline and instant creativity.

This conversational menu brings together different ideas and techniques which are surprising in their effect and their taste. It is a celebration-style of menu, so we have called it a birthday lunch buffet to capture this spirit. The ideas behind this menu are generous and worthy of friends. They suit an Australian setting, where people are generous about what they are prepared to try. We can picture these dishes on an alfresco table, the atmosphere drenched with warmth and bonhomie. You might choose to present one group of dishes first then follow it with another, each guest taking a little at a time to taste and savour and enjoy with conversation. The food is likely to inspire tales of travel—the time when we ate crab in Singapore, or closer to home, brandade at Berowra Waters. It is likely to remind us what bounty we have in our southern waters—who needs the Mediterranean after all?

Sunday Birthday Lunch Buffet recipes

SAFFRON FISH CONSOMMÉ WITH SALMON-ROE CREAM
AND TOASTED SHALLOT

SPICY FRIED CALAMARI MUGHLAI STYLE
WITH SWEET FRAGRANT RICE

OLIVE-FRIED GIANT SOUTHERN OCTOPUS
AND AVOCADO SALAD

DEEP-FRIED BRANDADE CUBES
WITH ELEPHANT EYES

NANJING SALAD

NONYA CHILLI MUD CRAB

PEKING-STYLE ROAST DUCK
WRAPPED IN LOTUS PANCAKE

BRAISED LAMB NECK WITH BEEF TENDON

ORANGE AND GRAND MARNIER SOUFFLÉ CAKE

Saffron fish consommé with salmon-roe cream and toasted shallot

I was amazed and delighted when travellers told me about salmon-roe cream. I did not have a recipe so I constructed one from their description and used shallots to enhance and offset the fish flavour, a typical Chinese ploy. The salmon roe is the exciting element in this soup because the heat from the clear stock explodes the roe in your mouth. One of my uncles, who is very much the Chinese gourmet, commented on this dish when he came to Neddy's. He called it 'lively', and I took that as a great compliment.

An Asian-style stock combined with a European clarification technique leads to a clear orange-coloured consommé which has superb flavour and great elegance. The toasted shallots are a Chinese favourite in soups, and work well in this instance, while the salmon-roe cream is the key to success. You will need six individual consommé cups. White cups will enhance the appearance of the consommé.

Consommé
Fish stock and farce
  for clarification (see page 221)

1 g packet or generous pinch of
  saffron strands

Toasted shallots
2½ tablespoons oil

3 shallots, sliced

Salmon-roe cream

120 ml crème fraîche   30 g salmon roe

Garnish

fresh coriander

Toasted shallots

Heat oil until it smokes then reduce to moderate heat and add sliced shallot, stirring to separate. As soon as the shallot turns golden, strain quickly and leave on kitchen paper to cool.

Salmon-roe cream

Lightly whip crème fraîche then fold in salmon roe.

Composition

Reheat the consommé. Add saffron strands and turn off the heat. Add equal portions of toasted shallots to each cup then pour in the consommé. Just before serving, ladle 1 tablespoon of salmon-roe cream into each cup and garnish with a coriander leaf. Consume at once.

Spicy fried calamari mughlai style with sweet fragrant rice

As a child I am introduced to mughlai or mogul cuisine. Not very far from my father's shop around the corner from the bus station is where the Indians do their trade—fragrant spices, copperware, chillis and onions drying out on nets—shops which always have a steep flight of steps at the front. Below the steps are the money lenders, above, the heavenly food. A nearby restaurant called the Taj Mahal is where my paternal aunt (who looks after me a lot of the time) takes me to eat banana, chutney, pickles, curry, rice, and the very best bread and curry puffs to be found.

The Taj Mahal is run by a maharajah's former chef. I am thirteen and my eighth uncle is going to have a birthday. He loves Indian food and decides that this chef must preside over the birthday dinner. The chef agrees. We are supplying the meat from our own farm—two goats are being fattened and forty chickens await their sacrifice. Now the birthday dinner has come and I see five mountains of biriani dishes, studded with the forty chickens and the twin goats, and jewelled with a hundred nuts, fruits and spices. My mother and I quite separately peel off from our groups—she from the adults and I from the children. Coincidentally, we are drawn at the same time to the kitchen to see the master at work. He shooes us away but not before we have laid *eyes on the huge pots heated by ground fire. The chef has his own personal box of spices and his apron is a mobile version of spice drawers—even his helpers do not know which spices he is using. He appears as a magician might, dispensing clouds of secret spices from his concealing gown into rich bubbling cauldrons. It is then that we realise that this man has honoured us by preparing this birthday dinner.*

Sweet fragrant rice

350 ml water
1 stick cinnamon
4 whole cloves
1 g saffron
1 fresh chilli, chopped

½ teaspoon turmeric powder
½ teaspoon cardamom seeds
280 g coconut cream
500 g long grain rice
½ teaspoon salt

Spicy fried calamari

500 g calamari pieces
1 teaspoon salt
½ tablespoon chilli powder
½ teaspoon ground turmeric
1 clove garlic, chopped
1 cm knob ginger, chopped
250 ml peanut oil

1 teaspoon cumin seeds
4 dried red chillies, whole
1 sprig curry leaves
2 tablespoons yoghurt
  (sheep or goat)
juice of 1 large lemon

Garnish

curry leaves
dried chillies

fresh mint

Sweet fragrant rice

Place water, cinnamon stick, cloves, saffron, chilli, turmeric powder, cardamom seeds and coconut cream in a pot and bring the mixture to the boil.

Add the rice and salt to the spice mixture and cook until the coconut cream has been completely absorbed by the rice.

Remove rice from the pot, place in a steamer and cook for 20 minutes, then stir. Cook for a further 20 minutes.

Spicy fried calamari

Season squid with salt, chilli powder and turmeric. Peel garlic and ginger and grind them together then add them to squid.

Heat oil and fry cumin seeds, whole dried chillies and curry leaves until brown. Add squid and yoghurt and fry until the squid starts to curl and the liquid has evaporated.

Composition

Sprinkle calamari with lemon juice before serving. Loosen and fluff the fragrant rice and place on a serving platter. Make a small well in the rice and fill it with the calamari. Garnish with the remaining curry leaves and dried chilli and top with fresh mint.

Olive-fried giant southern octopus and avocado salad

Reach for a tentacle, but make sure it's the right sort. The giant southern octopus is very different from the small Asian variety and should be used in this timeless dish. I was taught how to cook giant octopus by Christo, the Greek chef at The Iliad where I worked. The Greek way, of course, would be to use lemon and oregano as seasonings. Large octopus needs to be tumbled first by the fishmonger to relax the muscle, but a mallet, applied properly without damaging the meat, can be just as effective. The Greeks keep the skin on and I agree with this—it has a much stronger octopus flavour. The juice from the cooked octopus can be mixed with tomato sauce and balsamic vinegar, then tossed with pasta and a few octopus rings for a wonderful, wonderful dish. Too often these days we see octopus being served chargrilled, which is a pity.

This is a perfect dish for Adelaide's Mediterranean climate, although I'm not sure whether they ever had avocado in Greece. To complicate the geography, it makes me think of Kuala Lumpur and the Klang River where octopus and calamari are fried in a similar manner, but not, of course, with olives nor using this variety of octopus. Giant octopus tastes almost like lobster and is much nicer to eat—Greeks and Italians know this. In my mind the olives take the place of blachan and other South-East Asian spices, because they give an almost smoky flavour to this dish. At Neddy's this was a composition challenge because it had to go out looking like a bouquet, testing the willpower of the apprentices—it was impossible to rush and could not be prepared too far in advance. Tim Pak Poy, Julie Ziukelis and Lorraine Nelson were the apprentices at that time.

This dish is a Mediterranean 'romance', fitting for the Dunstan political era and the Adelaide arts mafia, who dallied with all things cosmopolitan. Avocado was very trendy in Adelaide when this dish was created, but at that time there was only one variety in the greengrocer's shop. Octopus was another 'new' ingredient for the Adelaide market; cheap then at $2 a kilo. It had been featured at a new Greek restaurant, The Iliad—the first popular ethnic restaurant of its type, catering for a multicultural clientele in Whitmore Square. A minor historical diversion seems right here: Whitmore Square is one of the many town squares devised in 1836 by the town planner, Colonel William Light, son of an Englishman, Frances Light (who planned Penang) and a Malay princess. Whether William was planned we will never know but we in Adelaide appreciate his realised vision of wide streets and parklands in a gracious city.

Octopus

1 litre olive oil	4 fresh chillies
200 g black olives, slightly crushed	2.5 kg octopus
2 whole bulbs garlic, cut in half horizontally	1 bay leaf

Salad

2 grapefruit	50 g capers
1 Spanish onion, thinly sliced	plain flour
40 g sun-dried tomatoes	olive oil
2 heads frisée lettuce	2 avocados

Dressing

3 tablespoons virgin olive oil	freshly ground black pepper
1 clove garlic, crushed	2 tablespoons dry white wine
1 tablespoon Dijon mustard	1 teaspoon sugar
juice of 2 lemons	

Octopus

Put the olive oil in a large pot and heat until smoking. Add crushed olives, garlic and chillies and bring oil back to smoking point. Gather the octopus by the tentacles and gently lower it head first into the hot oil to seal it evenly. You might need to immerse each octopus individually. Once they are all sealed put them all back in the oil. Add the bay leaf then cover the pot and reduce the flame to a gentle simmer—as low as possible. Simmer for 45 minutes to 1 hour. Allow the octopus to cool in the juice then reduce by one-third for later use.

Salad

Peel the skin and membrane off the grapefruit. Using a sharp knife, cut down one side of the membrane between each segment and flip the segment out, removing the seeds at the same time. Mix grapefruit, onion, sun-dried tomatoes and frisée lettuce. Roll the capers in flour, deep-fry and set aside. Slice avocado into thin slices.

Dressing

Combine dressing ingredients and mix with the salad.

Composition

Arrange slices of avocado on the centre of a serving platter. Place sliced octopus on top of the avocado and the salad on top of the octopus. Drizzle a spoonful of the octopus juice around the plate and garnish with fried capers.

Deep-fried brandade cubes with elephant eyes

The Chinese believe elephant eyes bring good fortune, but relax, no illegal game hunting is required—this is a trompe l'oeil dish. The eyes are in fact halved pigeon eggs garnished with ham to form an ocular illusion.

The brandade cubes are prepared using mashed salted cod that must first be soaked in several changes of fresh water for 24 hours. This softens the fish to an almost fresh state, and desalinates it. Once prepared, the cube mixture must be chilled overnight to firm it for cutting, so allow at least 36 hours for this dish. The cubes and the eyes are deep-fried just before serving. The sauce can be prepared before this last step.

Brandade cubes
1 kg dried, split, salted cod
2 slices lemon
1 large onion, sliced
500 ml milk
6 stalks parsley, chopped
250 g desirée potatoes
2 cloves garlic, finely chopped
2 tablespoons Italian parsley leaves,
   finely chopped

3 hard-boiled eggs, shelled
   and sliced
3 fresh eggs
225 ml walnut oil, warmed
1 teaspoon sea salt
1 teaspoon freshly crushed
   peppercorn

Cube crumbs
1 egg
500 ml milk
½ teaspoon salt
½ teaspoon white pepper

200 g plain flour
250 g white breadcrumbs
olive oil

Elephant eyes
6 pigeon eggs, hard-boiled
   and shelled
60 g green prawns
60 g pork fillet
1 teaspoon rice wine
½ teaspoon salt
1 teaspoon sugar
½ teaspoon sesame oil
1 eggwhite

1 teaspoon cornflour
1 teaspoon finely chopped ginger
1 teaspoon finely chopped spring
   onion, white only
6 slices white bread
1½ tablespoons finely chopped
   smoked ham
peanut oil

Tomato and garlic sauce

1 tablespoon olive oil
1 small onion, finely chopped
4 cloves garlic, finely chopped
10 tomatoes, skinned, halved
  and seeded

1 tablespoon sugar
150 ml dry white wine (Noilly Prat)
1 sprig thyme
1 sprig tarragon
½ bay leaf

Garnish

deep-fried celery leaves

Brandade cubes

Soak the cod in cold water for 24 hours changing the water several times. With a very sharp knife, slice cod then pound it with a hammer to loosen the meat. Put the fish pieces, lemon slices, onion, milk and parsley stalks in a large saucepan, cover with water and bring to the boil. Simmer for 15–20 minutes then allow to cool in the broth. Strain and reserve the broth. Break the fish into flakes, removing bones and skin. Pound flesh with a mortar and pestle, or mash in a food processor, until smooth.

Peel potatoes and boil them in the cod broth, then mash and strain them through a drum sieve and reheat in a saucepan. Add mashed cod, garlic, parsley leaves and hard-boiled eggs. Lightly whisk the three eggs with the warm walnut oil and incorporate into the hot mashed potato. Season with the salt and pepper.

Pour this mixture into a lightly oiled tray until 3–4 cm deep. Chill overnight. Unmould and cut into 3–4 cm cubes.

Cube crumbs

Lightly whisk egg and milk and season with the salt and pepper. Dust cubes with flour then individually roll in the eggwash, then the bread-crumbs. Chill in the refrigerator for 1 hour.

Heat olive oil and deep-fry cubes before serving.

Elephant eyes

Cut pigeon eggs in half lengthwise. Finely mince prawns and pork together then add rice wine, salt, sugar, sesame oil, eggwhite, cornflour, ginger and spring onion and chill for 30 minutes. Trim the crusts off the bread and cut each slice in 5 cm wide strips and then into diamond shapes by making parallel diagonal cuts along the length. Discard the end pieces. Place pigeon egg flat side down on the diamond and spread pork and prawn mixture around the egg to form the 'elephant eye'. Place chopped ham in the two 'corners' of each eye. The mixture will stick to the bread and stay intact during frying.

Just before serving, heat oil in a wok over medium heat and deep-fry the 'eyes' until crisp; use a metal ladle to gently roll the 'eyes' in the oil to ensure even cooking. At this point, also deep-fry the celery leaves for garnish.

Tomato and garlic sauce

Preheat the oven to 160°C. Heat the oil in an ovenproof dish and sauté the onion and garlic. Stir in the tomatoes, sugar and then white wine and herbs. Cover with a piece of greaseproof paper and cook in the oven for 1 hour. Strain through a fine sieve. If you wish, you can add a little more olive oil at this point.

Composition

Ladle the tomato and garlic sauce onto the centre of a shallow serving dish. Arrange the brandade cubes and elephant eyes on the sides of the plate. Garnish with the deep-fried celery leaves.

Nanjing salad

In China, with my father, the plane is late arriving at the Nanjing airport—an army-style airfield where we are ushered through a type of bunker and then through immigration. We arrive at the small hotel around 10 pm, hungry and worried that dinner might not be served. We are catered for, but the dinner is very poor. The soup is described as a clear, clean, fresh pork soup. We laugh when one of the guests says it is so clear and fresh it tastes like water. Next day, by way of apology, the manager treats us to a special banquet. The first dish to come out is this one—a salad of pickled vegetables combined with fresh fruits. I like it very much and serve my own version at Neddy's when I come home. Another discovery is the most famous Nanjing dish—saltwater duck. I learn how to cook it in Nanjing, with the advice of our tour-leader who is very interested in cuisine. I put this duck on top of the salad at Neddy's, and Maggie Beer likes it so much that she serves saltwater duck at the Pheasant Farm. Our team presents saltwater duck for the award-winning Seppelts Australian Menu of the Year in 1992. Then it travels to New York when we present our dishes there as the Australian champions...

Half the guests in the hotel at Nanjing that night are Japanese visitors—they came because Nanjing is famous for calligraphy, a prized art in Japan and China. They are buying the best brushes, and the ink—you buy it in slabs—is like stone.

Salad

1 tablespoon salt
2 medium continental cucumbers,
  peeled, seeded and thinly sliced
3 medium carrots, cut into julienne
4 tablespoons rice vinegar

3 blood oranges
½ pineapple, cut into cubes
1 fresh red chilli, seeded and sliced
¼ cup mint, finely chopped

Salt the cucumber and carrots. Allow to stand in a bowl for 30 minutes then add vinegar and stand for a further 30 minutes. Strain and dry.

Peel the skin and membrane off the oranges. Using a sharp knife, cut down one side of the membrane between each segment and flip the segment out, removing the seeds at the same time.

Mix together the pineapple, orange fillets and chilli. Mix in with the cucumber and carrots. Add fresh mint.

Nonya chilli mud crab

Chilli crab under the Klang bridge—the port is famous for it. Father would drive my grandmother there to eat chilli crab. I learnt this dish from my mother. She always tells me that crab must be cooked perfectly—too much and it will lose texture; too little and it will be unpleasant to eat. When I first saw blue swimmer crabs here I was shocked to see they were sold dead. In Asia they are always sold alive. Blue swimmer is tastier but the mud crab has more meat. When I first bought mud crab in Australia it was very expensive—around $16 per kilo—and very few restaurants bought it. It was always difficult to cover costs and there was the dilemma of trying to convince Australians to eat with their fingers, especially with a sauce. Fortunately at Neddy's there was a racehorse vet who used to come and ask for chilli crab and a local winemaker who also liked this dish. A yes or no depended on availability so I did not put it on the menu. Also the customers then could not cope with eating it in the shell; now there is greater understanding. I served Derek Nimmo the same style of dish using prawns and he enjoyed it—but shelling the complete prawns was a challenge for him. Julie Ziukelis used crab often at Bijou in Adelaide. Chinese add to nonya cuisine by using lard, enhancing and sealing in the fragrance of the crab.

This is a hot, spicy, exotic, tasty, 'agony and ecstasy' dish, with biting chilli and wonderful flavour. Asian cookery involves all the senses—hearing, sight, touch, taste and smell. This dish explains the interaction between at least three—try listening to the good oil.

Crabs are best bought cooked in Australia provided you can buy them on the same day. The next day they will have deteriorated and are not worth buying. If you buy them alive they should be very active; if slow, they are dehydrated and will be dry when cooked. Mud crab is always sold alive. Blue swimmer crab is a good substitute if mud crab is not available.

2 large mud crabs, live
½ tablespoon ginger juice
½ tablespoon spring onion juice
80 g lard
1 tablespoon oil
1 tablespoon rice wine
8 shallots, finely sliced
4 cloves garlic, finely chopped
1 cm knob ginger, finely chopped

2 tablespoons brown bean paste
1 tablespoon blachan
1 dried chilli, finely chopped
2 fresh chillies, seeded and
  finely chopped
2 teaspoons light soy sauce
2 tablespoons sugar
spring onion, shredded
fresh coriander

Kill the crabs by plunging a sharp knife between the eyes; death is instant. Shell each crab and using a brush, clean off any mud or sand. Cut into six pieces and lightly crack the claws. Marinate with the ginger and spring onion juices.

Heat lard in a wok and lightly fry the crab pieces until cooked. Set aside and remove fat from the wok. Add oil to the wok and fry the remaining ingredients except soy sauce and sugar, until the crackling sound of the oil starts to reduce and you can hear only the odd crackle. Now add the soy sauce and sugar. Stir in the crab pieces and cook for a further two minutes. If it becomes too dry add a little water.

Composition

Place crab and sauce on a plate and garnish with spring onion and fresh coriander.

Peking-style roast duck wrapped in lotus pancake

At Neddy's this was my version (and Adelaide's first experience) of Peking duck—a discovery of skin and fat and the pleasing sharpness of raw spring onion. I sometimes think of it as a Chinese version of Greek lamb yiros. We used to cook the duck in a metal olive-shaped oven which was at the end of the courtyard, hanging the bird vertically with a duck hook. Fruit wood was used as fuel in the centre of the oven; usually one oven load of wood cooked the ducks perfectly. Eighteen ducks could be prepared in this way at one go.

In Beijing they once used domed brick ovens with vertical flues and fired them with fruit wood—now the ovens are all electric. The rearing of the ducks is what imparts the flavour. They are fed on corn and sorghum intensively for two weeks before killing, so that the meat is heavily marbled and the skin is thick.

The method of preparation is similar to that used in the recipe for Loquat Mandolin-shaped Duck. Once again, the success of this dish is based on the skin. To make this cooking experience even more novel, you will need to arm yourself with a bicycle pump and a long funnel, or use an electric air compressor.

Duck

2.2–2.4 kg duck, Peking
  variety (look for perfect skin,
  no bruises or tears)
1 tablespoon prickly ash
1 tablespoon Kaoliang wine

1 spring onion
1 star anise
1 clove garlic, crushed
1 slice fresh ginger
2½ tablespoons maltose

needle and string or fine skewer
  to seal duck cavity

bicycle pump
funnel

Lotus pancake

see Red Bean Paste Pancakes,
  page 144

hoi sin sauce

Garnish

cucumber, cut into fingers

spring onion, white only, cut into
  5 cm lengths

Duck

Using a tea-towel or kitchen paper clean the cavity of the duck, remove wing tips and any offal remaining in the cavity, then rub the cavity with prickly ash.

Sprinkle the wine into the cavity and insert the spring onion, star anise, garlic and ginger close to the very end of the opening. Close up the opening with either a needle and string or a fine skewer, sealing it tight. (I use blanket stitch to prevent any liquid leaking from the cavity.)

Insert the tube of the pump between the neck skin and flesh and hold tube and skin together tightly. Pump air under the skin to separate it from the meat. Inflate until the skin lifts off the duck (this will help to make the skin crisp when roasted). Remove the pump and tie the neck quickly with string to keep in the air.

Bring a kettle to the boil then wait for the water to cool slightly. Pour water over the duck until the skin tightens. (The water forms a protective seal which conserves the juices during roasting.) Mix the maltose with half a cup of water and brush over the duck. Hang the duck in a well-ventilated space for 12 hours or in front of a fan for 4 hours. Remove string.

Preheat the oven to 220°C. Place the narrow end of the funnel in the neck opening. Bring 3 cups of water to the boil and pour the water through the funnel. Using string, close up the neck as tightly as possible so that the water can't flow out. (This keeps the duck moist and shortens the cooking time.) Place duck on a rack and roast in the oven for 45 minutes, turning it over halfway through.

Lotus pancake

Divide the dough into walnut-sized pieces using the same dividing technique described on page 66 and roll into a disc about the size of a saucer. Pan-fry without oil, almost a grilling method, until the pancake puffs up. If you are familiar with chapatis you will recognise exactly when they are ready; they should be white.

Composition

Using a very sharp knife, remove the duck skin with at least 4 mm of meat attached. Brush the lotus pancake with some hoi sin sauce and place on it one finger of cucumber and some spring onion white. Place the duck skin on top and roll up the pancake. Each diner can roll their own at the table or the pancakes can be wrapped and placed around the carved remainder of the duck on a serving plate.

Braised lamb neck with beef tendon

South Australian lamb is excellent and this dish is very fitting for a city such as Adelaide which prides itself on good eating and relaxed hospitality. The best lamb for this dish comes from northern South Australia, where the stock feeds on vast tracts of semi-desert saltbush. This lamb, and that of Kangaroo Island, most closely resembles the famous pré-salé (salt field) lamb of France. Prepare the beef tendon well in advance. You can buy it from Chinese grocery shops.

Beef tendon
250 g beef tendon	slice of ginger
peanut oil	1 spring onion

Lamb
1 kg lamb neck	1 dried red chilli, whole
200 g butter	3 tomatoes
salt	1 teaspoon orange zest
freshly ground black pepper	10–12 baby onions, whole
3 tablespoons white wine,	100 g baby carrots, whole
chardonnay	3 tablespoons mineral water
1 bay leaf	100 g shiitake mushrooms
6 cloves garlic, sliced	kitchen string

Beef tendon

Submerge the beef tendon in *cold* peanut oil (enough to cover the meat). Heat up over a very low flame. When the oil is hot, the beef tendon will float to the top and double in size. Remove from the oil and place in a pot of cold water with the ginger and spring onion. Bring to the boil then refresh under cold water.

Lamb

Preheat the oven to 160°C. Skin, seed and dice the tomatoes. Truss the lamb neck with kitchen string. Heat one-third of the butter in a large, heavy pot with a lid and brown the lamb on all sides over a high heat. Season with salt and pepper. Remove lamb and deglaze the pot with the white wine then add bay leaf, garlic, chilli, tomatoes and orange zest and cook for a few minutes. Arrange the prepared beef tendon around the lamb neck and cover with the lid. Cook in the oven for 2 hours, turning occasionally and checking that there is sufficient moisture. Add a few spoonfuls of water if necessary. Add the onions halfway through the cooking period.

Clean and peel the baby carrots. Heat most of the remaining butter in a pan, reserving a cube, and lightly cook the carrots for a few minutes. Add the mineral water, season with salt and pepper and cook for 5 minutes. Toss in the shiitake mushrooms. Add this mixture to the lamb at the last moment.

Composition

Place carrots, onions, mushrooms and beef tendon on a serving plate. Strain cooking liquid into a saucepan and whisk in the cube of butter without allowing it to boil. Pour over the lamb or serve separately in a sauce boat.

Orange and Grand Marnier soufflé cake

*This dessert expresses Mary's love for Italian desserts which she thinks
are very suited to the Asian palate. Intense sweetness contrasts with
the bitter zest. This recipe requires the pulp of whole oranges and is
cooked like a soufflé. The original recipe does not use a rising agent
and is therefore heavier and richer. Hardy Jecher, master pâtissier at
Regency Hotel School, refined this recipe to allow students to present
a simpler and lighter dessert without loss of character.*

Soufflé cake

3 oranges

100 ml Grand Marnier

8 eggs, separated

265 g sugar

1 teaspoon baking powder

400 g blanched walnut meal

400 g orange marmalade, strained
to remove rind

Garnish

candied orange zest

¼ cup flaked almonds, roasted

mascarpone or clotted cream

Clean and boil the oranges for 2 hours. Allow oranges to cool then purée
skin and flesh. Add Grand Marnier to taste.

Preheat the oven to 190°C. Over a pot of simmering water, make a
sabayon with the egg yolks and 200 g of the sugar, then whisk to cool.

Beat eggwhites until soft peaks form. Sift together the baking powder and
walnut meal and add remaining sugar. Fold the orange purée and the
sifted dry ingredients alternately into the sabayon. Fold in the eggwhites.

Divide evenly into two 22 cm cake rings and bake for approximately
55 minutes.

To glaze, bring the marmalade to the boil and pour over the cake.

Composition

 Finish the sides of the cake with roasted flaked almonds and
garnish with julienne of candied orange zest. Serve with a dollop
of fresh mascarpone or clotted cream.

Simple Chinese Home Menu

Learning how to shop in the market is the skill behind all home menus—it accounts for half the talent of cooking. I was fortunate to learn this skill from my grandma and aunties. To choose the freshest vegetables, check the stem for woodiness and fibre. If it is dry, it has been cut too long ago. Check the leaves to see that they are not infested with insects, the veins are not too large, showing age, and the colour is brilliant. To choose poultry, look at the feathers to see how old the bird is. Check the tail feathers—if the feather pins are hard and prominent then the bird is getting old. Fish should only be bought when absolutely fresh, preferably live; it should be firm to the touch, brilliant in colour, with clear eyes and skin that is slimy, not dry. For meat, a trustworthy butcher is the first requirement, learning the appropriate cuts for certain dishes is the second. Buying groceries takes much practice and one relies upon information from others— which brands of sauce are the best; which dry goods are reliable.

When you prepare this menu note the practical aspects. The stock from the steeped chicken could be used as a soup with Chinese greens. The duck could be prepared in advance and reheated. The steamed fish takes only 3–5 minutes to cook. The menu relies on planning, preparation and timing, but much can be achieved that is satisfying, healthy, tasty and balanced without major effort.

Adelaide's market is called the Central Market and that is exactly what it is. Easy to get to—like much of Adelaide—it concentrates people and cultures. People at the Adelaide market—from stall holders to shoppers—will share their knowledge. If a person sees you buying an ingredient that is unfamiliar to them, they will generally ask you for advice. There is none of the impersonality of the supermarket, and its central city site makes it a meeting place on Friday nights and Saturday mornings. Australians of Asian descent may visit the market as often as three times a week, and in many parts of Asia people shop daily, especially where there is little refrigeration. In the Adelaide of only fifteen years ago there were few Asian ingredients and little fresh produce. If friends were going to Melbourne they would often be asked to bring back a roast duck or some 'obscure' Chinese dry ingredients. These days there is an abundance of Chinese ingredients available, and much of the produce is grown or made in Australia: fresh beancurd and noodles, snow-pea shoots and many other greens, pickles, sausages, air-dried meat goods, bread and cakes, yum cha dim sum, pig's blood and fish balls, even yellow corn-fed chickens complete with head and feet—anathema to the supermarketers.

The appearance of live animals has been limited to fish in tanks and live poultry. Whether Australian markets will ever stock other live produce for the table remains to be seen. That would mean facing the reality that the supermarket disguises. Of greater concern is the threat to the corner butcher shop—once an Australian institution—where the butcher offers advice and suggestions and will cut according to the customer's needs. Relying on prepared supermarket pre-cut meat takes us even further away from the knowledge and the quality that is essential to good cooking and eating.

The simplicity of spring onion and ginger, suppressing strong odours and adding aromatic fragrance; the importance of fresh ingredients; the balance of green vegetable for digestion, a small portion of meat for strength, fresh fish for energy, and soup for warmth and nourishment—every Chinese household cook will have this balance in mind when they prepare the family meal. There is no need to consult diet specialists, but a herbalist may prescribe some special tonic soup for healing. Yin and Yang: in winter there may be game to heat the blood and ward off chills; in summer there will be cooling tonics to counteract the heat.

Bringing the family together to eat and to share the food placed in the centre of the table symbolises the strength of the family as a unit. The oldest will start eating first, murmuring 'sic fan' (eat rice)—a signal to all others to start. One person may leave more of a dish for another and all will take care to eat in such a way that nobody misses out. Mothers may peel back the crispy skin from the fried fish (the favourite part) and place it on their child's plate with their chopsticks. The young will make sure that the old have most of the 'hottest' dishes to ward off the cold.

If you are a guest at a Chinese table remember to take enough for the first mouthful and repeat the process—that way all will be shared. Remember, too, that the meats and vegetables are accompaniments to the rice. Take plenty of rice—the dishes are for all and you should not concentrate on only one but take a little from each. You should turn the plate around if you want to take from the other end of the dish, but only when everyone else has had their turn. Never stretch across to take from the furthest end of the plate; on the other hand, whatever is nearest to you on the plate is free for you to enjoy.

Simple Chinese Home Menu recipes

STEAMED ATLANTIC SALMON FILLET
WITH SPRING ONIONS AND CORIANDER

PERFECT STEEPED WHITE CHICKEN

RED-ROAST CALLOP WITH GREENS, SPRING ONION
AND CORIANDER SAUCE

GREEN CHOY SUM WITH WHITE-BAIT STOCK

LAMB OR GOAT CASSEROLE WITH RED DATES,
WATER CHESTNUTS AND WOOD FUNGUS

CRISP STUFFED EGGPLANT SALAD

STEAMED JASMINE-SCENTED WHITE RICE

RED BEAN PASTE PANCAKES

Steamed Atlantic salmon fillet with spring onions and coriander

Living in Australia we can have the luxury of using this fish—it is out of reach for many in other parts of the world. Wonderfully delicate, slightly oily, and always able to be obtained fresh, this fish lends itself to the Chinese approach and is economical because the slices are quite thick and a couple of pieces is enough for a family of six.

How can a couple of pieces suffice? Because this will be one dish among several—served as part of a meal in which rice is the staple. The idea is not to have fish with rice but to have rice with fish. This is an important aspect of Chinese etiquette.

Steam gently for a very brief time. This simple but elegant dish can be completed very quickly for a dinner party.

Steamed Salmon

1 kg Atlantic salmon, skin left
  on, rib bones removed
salt
freshly ground black pepper
2 teaspoons rice wine
6 spring onions, finely shredded,
  white and green separated

2 cm knob ginger, finely shredded
3 tablespoons white chicken stock
  (see page 224)
1 tablespoon light soy sauce
1 teaspoon sugar
3 tablespoons peanut oil
fresh coriander

Steamed Salmon

Season salmon with salt, pepper and half the rice wine. Place salmon in a Chinese steamer and steam over a gentle heat for about 3 minutes—the meat should still be pink. Strain off the juices. Place the fish on a serving dish, then cover with the shredded spring onion (white only, reserve the green) and ginger.

Bring the stock to the boil, remove from the heat and add soy sauce, remaining rice wine and sugar and pour this over the salmon. Heat the oil in a pan until smoking, add the green of the spring onion then pour over the fish.

Composition

 Garnish the serving plate with fresh coriander and serve immediately.

Perfect steeped white chicken

A wonderfully versatile chicken dish: the meat can be used in salads, eaten cold or hot, or carved into slices in the traditional Chinese manner and served with a dipping sauce of soy, oil, shallot, ginger and spring onion. The meat is tender, succulent and delectable and the white and red parts are distinctly coloured. The poaching method using hot as opposed to simmering stock ensures that the breast meat is not tough or stringy, the great test for any whole chicken dish. The shallot and ginger offset the metallic taste which is sometimes present in plain poached chicken. A little red blood in the centre of the chicken bones is acceptable, otherwise the cooking time would be too long for the meat. To ensure a perfectly finished dish, the lifting and re-submerging of the chicken must be done without breaking the skin.

Drizzling soy sauce and warm peanut oil over the meat pieces will add to the flavour if you do not have time to prepare the dipping sauce. Peeled cucumber slices on the base of the plate adds colour and a taste and texture contrast. Country people, who eat mainly rice, use dipping sauces to add flavour to their meals.

Steeped chicken
1.8 kg chicken, preferably very fresh Kangaroo Island corn-fed	1 tablespoon rice wine
1 tablespoon salt	5 litres white chicken stock (see page 224)
1 tablespoon light soy sauce	1 slice ginger (extra)
1 cm knob ginger	1 spring onion stalk (extra)
1 spring onion, pounded together with the ginger	

Dipping sauce
2 cm knob ginger	1 tablespoon light soy sauce
2 spring onions, white only	1 tablespoon shallot oil

Garnish
sliced spring onion

Steeped chicken

Season the chicken cavity with salt, soy sauce, ginger, spring onion and rice wine and leave aside for 1 hour.

Fill a large pot with water and bring to the boil. It is essential that the chicken be fully immersed at all stages to ensure thorough cooking. Blanch the chicken, 1 minute at a time, a couple of times, carefully lifting it in and out of the pot under the wing, so as not to bruise the skin. This process of 'changing the water' washes the salted cavity of excess blood and impurities, and at the same time, seals the cavity. Remove the chicken, and refresh it in very cold water to firm the flesh and seal the skin.

In another pot, bring chicken stock to the boil with the slice of ginger and spring onion stalk then lower the chicken gently into the stock with a carving fork just under the chicken wing, taking care not to bruise the skin. Repeat the same lifting and submerging process used during the blanching process, this time to heat the cavity, which will be less cooked than the exterior. Then submerge the chicken completely in the stock.

Bring the stock to the boil, skimming off any impurities. Remove the pot from the stove and allow the chicken to steep in the stock for 25 minutes. Remove the chicken gently from the pot and place it on a serving dish to cool for 30 minutes. By this time the bird is fully rested and is ready for slicing.

Dipping sauce

Pound ginger and spring onion to a paste, add soy sauce and shallot oil.

Composition

 Serve chicken on a serving plate, cut in either Chinese or Western style. Garnish with the sliced spring onion. Place dipping sauce on the side.

Red-roast callop with greens, spring onion and coriander sauce

This is a dish that demonstrates one of the most important principles of Chinese cuisine: a place for everything and everything in its place *before any cooking is commenced.*

Preparation and organisation is essential for proper timing and to achieve the right effect for many Chinese dishes. I place each ingredient in its own container and mix the sauce ingredients in advance so that the sequence can be exact. In this dish the cooking time is only 5–7 minutes, so the timing is critical. One missed ingredient, or the order changed and the result will not be as good. Make the effort to prepare carefully and attend to the logical sequence and you will be rewarded.

A pungent dish replete with the perfume of coriander and celery, the peppery flavour of green chillies and a rich sauce. The golden perch looks as if it has been roasted with a firm texture, but it should be evenly cooked, moist right to the bone. This is the perfect treatment for a freshwater fish like Murray River callop. The meat might be too oily for the Anglo-Australian palate which is accustomed to finer textured flesh. For those of other cultural backgrounds, especially Asia, the texture is highly prized for its delicate smoothness. The oil of the fish and the sauce are perfectly matched in this Peking-style dish.

Marinade

1 tablespoon soy sauce
1 stalk spring onion, finely chopped
1 cm knob ginger, finely chopped
1 tablespoon rice wine

1 teaspoon sugar
pinch of salt
pinch of white pepper
1 tablespoon oil

Sauce

1 tablespoon oyster sauce
½ tablespoon dark soy sauce

½ tablespoon light soy sauce

Red-roast callop

1 whole callop
1 teaspoon salt
1 shallot
1 clove garlic, finely chopped
1 cm knob ginger, finely chopped
   or grated
1 stalk celery

4 spring onions, green only
3 green chillies
250 ml sunflower oil (or grapeseed)
1 teaspoon rice wine
150 ml white chicken stock
   (see page 224)

Garnish

1 tablespoon chopped fresh
   coriander

extra spring onion, shredded

Marinade

Mix together marinade ingredients and marinate callop for 30 minutes. This will bring out the natural flavour rather than overpowering it.

Sauce

Mix oyster sauce and soy sauce in a bowl to make the seasoning sauce.

Red-roast callop

Chop shallot, garlic, ginger, celery, spring onion and green chilli finely (no bigger than the size of a pin head) and set aside separately. Heat enough oil for shallow-frying in a large frying-pan or wok until smoking. Fry callop on both sides until brown—one minute per side. Take care not to damage the skin. Lift out the fish and place on kitchen paper. Remove the oil from the pan or wok and then add some hot water. Bring this to the boil and discard to clean the pan and prepare it for the braising stage.

Add a little spoon of oil to the pan and heat till barely smoking then add in this order: salt, finely chopped shallot, garlic and ginger and fry until pale golden. Then add finely chopped celery, spring onion and green chilli, and fry until the oil begins to separate from the ingredients. Flame with rice wine then add seasoning sauce and chicken stock. Add the fried fish and cook gently, turning until the eyes begin to pop—usually after about 7 minutes—then lift out. Place the fish on a serving dish.

Reduce the remaining liquid until the oil separates from the sauce, and taste for seasoning.

Composition

 Pour the sauce over the fish and garnish with coriander and spring onion.

Green choy sum with white-bait stock

A combination the Chinese would call 'precious'. A delectably clean stock, clear and without any trace of oiliness, accompanied by lightly cooked yet tender greens. Eating this dish gives one a feeling of well-being and comfort and so it is enjoyed by Chinese families as a restorative. You will find choy sum in Chinese grocery shops or in certain greengrocers.

2 bunches choy sum
50 g dried white bait, washed,
  heads and backbones removed

1 slice ginger
2 cloves garlic
1 tablespoon shallot oil

Wash choy sum thoroughly, especially towards the base of the vegetable as sand tends to collect there. Cut the leaves away from the stalk and keep them separate as the stalks require slightly longer cooking time.

Bring 2 litres of water to the boil. Add cleaned white bait, ginger and garlic cloves and simmer for 20 minutes. Remove from heat and allow to steep for a further 30 minutes. Strain the stock thoroughly through a fine sieve then bring back to the boil. Add the choy sum stalks first and simmer for about 5 minutes, then add the leaves until they turn a bright green colour, about another 2 minutes.

Composition

Lift the vegetables out of the stock and place on a serving plate. Spoon shallot oil over them. Serve the stock in individual small Chinese bowls— cockerel bowls to be truly traditional.

Lamb or goat casserole with red dates, water chestnuts and wood fungus

A family dish in the 'hunter's style' from my grandmother's time—the red dates intensify the sweetness of the dish but you could use figs to achieve the same soothing, balanced feeling. Time-honoured Chinese ingredients give it the salty, sweet and fruity flavour combination that is so highly prized.

This is a Peking-style dish in which the goat or lamb is cooked with fermented bean curd and brown beans. The people from the south of China dislike the rank flavour of goat and lamb. Perhaps it is the extreme cold of the north that makes this style of dish popular, or simply the Mongolian influence. The wood fungus absorbs all the flavour from the meat and becomes soft and velvety. The goat's encasing membrane should be left on.

Meat
500 g shoulder of lamb or goat

Marinade
½ tablespoon ginger juice
½ tablespoon spring onion juice
1 tablespoon light soy sauce
pinch of salt
pinch of freshly ground black pepper

Casserole
200 g daikon
40 g water chestnuts (fresh Northern Territory variety are best, Maling tinned variety is a reasonable substitute)
2 red dates
peanut oil
1 tablespoon sesame oil
1 star anise
2 knobs ginger, finely chopped
1 bunch fresh coriander, roots and leaves, finely chopped
1 clove garlic, finely chopped
1 tablespoon white fermented bean curd
1 tablespoon brown bean paste
3 tablespoons soy sauce
2 tablespoons rice wine
1 piece dried tangerine peel, soaked, white pulp removed
1 packet wood fungus, soaked
500 ml white chicken stock (see page 224)
2 spring onions
2 tablespoons sugar

Meat

Cut meat into 3 cm cubes.

Marinade

Combine marinade ingredients. Add marinade to meat and set aside for 30 minutes.

Casserole

Peel the daikon and cut into 3 cm pieces, about the size of a fifty cent piece. Using a potato peeler, skin the fresh water chestnuts, taking care not to remove too much flesh. Wash and pat dry. (The tinned variety just need to be dried). Soak red dates for 20 minutes and remove seeds.

Bring a pot of water to the boil and blanch the meat in hot water for a few minutes, then refresh in cold water.

In a large casserole pot, heat enough oil to cover the base of the pot and brown the meat evenly then remove and place on kitchen paper to absorb the oil.

Remove excess oil from the pot. Add sesame oil, star anise, half of the ginger, coriander roots (reserve leaves for garnish), garlic, bean curd and brown bean paste and fry until fragrant. Add in the soy sauce and rice wine then stir in the meat. Add in red dates, tangerine peel, soaked and drained wood fungus and enough stock to cover the meat, and simmer for 1 hour, stirring occasionally to avoid burning the bottom layer.

Add in water chestnuts and daikon then simmer for 30 minutes, or until the pot is almost dry. Add the spring onion, sugar and remaining ginger 5 minutes before serving.

Composition

 Place on serving plate and garnish with the fresh coriander leaves.

Crisp stuffed eggplant salad

I like the balance of my simple home menu, which has fish, vegetables and meat. This dish has all three. The eggplant is crisp, which encourages children to try it and finally to appreciate it.

An appetising dish of eggplant stuffed with prawns and meat, finished with a rich sauce of brown bean paste, garlic and vinegar. The cucumber and tomato garnish provides a light and refreshing contrast. Choose the long Asian variety of eggplant available at Chinese groceries, in preference to the larger variety which has too many seeds.

Batter

70 g plain flour
225 g cornflour
2 whole eggs

½ cup water
3 tablespoons oil

Eggplant

500 g Asian eggplant
  (long and thin)
salt
150 g fresh tiger prawns
3 cm knob ginger, chopped
2 spring onions
150 g loin of pork, finely minced

2 teaspoons salt
1 teaspoon sugar
50 g pork back fat, finely diced
cornflour
peanut oil
3 cloves garlic, chopped
1 tablespoon soy bean paste

Seasoning

½ teaspoon salt
1 tablespoon sugar
1 tablespoon light soy sauce
2 tablespoons rice wine vinegar

2½ tablespoons water
½ teaspoon cornflour
1 tablespoon sesame oil
2 teaspoons rice wine

Garnish

chopped tomatoes and cucumber

Batter

Sieve flour and cornflour together. Lightly whisk eggs with the water. Add in oil. Gently mix the flour and egg mixtures together. Take care not to overwork the batter.

Eggplant

Cut eggplant diagonally into slices about 2 cm thick. Slice eggplant pieces horizontally through the centre, leaving a 'hinge' on one side so they look rather like opening mouths. Lightly salt and set aside.

Mince prawns, half the ginger and half the spring onions together. Place pork loin mince in a mixer and using a paddle, mix for one minute then add prawn mixture, 2 teaspoons salt and sugar and blend for a minute before adding diced pork fat last. (If the fat was added earlier it would prevent the blending of the other ingredients; the pork loin mince needs to be worked most of all.)

Gently open each eggplant 'mouth' without breaking the joined end, dust with cornflour and spread the mixture in between the eggplant. Dust the stuffed eggplant with cornflour and dip into the batter and deep-fry in hot oil until golden brown. Reheat in oil again for 10 seconds before arranging on a serving plate.

Heat a little oil in a frying pan and stir-fry chopped garlic and soy bean paste. Add the remaining chopped spring onions and ginger.

Seasoning

Combine seasoning ingredients and add to frying-pan. Bring to the boil and pour over the crisp eggplant. Garnish with tomato and cucumber.

Steamed jasmine-scented white rice

Rice—one of the staffs of life. At Chinese banquets where rice is not traditionally served as an accompaniment to the dishes, a rice dish, usually fried, will often appear on its own serving plate at the end of the meal. If anyone takes so much as a spoonful the rule is that it must be eaten up by those at the table until finished. This is a reminder that despite the rich dishes, rice is the most important food for life and it should never be wasted.

Use a good quality long-grain rice—in this case, jasmine scented. Australian varieties are generally of very high quality. First wash the rice to remove any dust and excess starch. To each cup of rice (you need around ½ to 1 cup per person depending on appetite) add 1¼ cups of water—that is the secret. Bring to the boil, cover tightly and turn to the lowest flame. After about 15-20 minutes from boiling point check to see that all the water has been absorbed and the grain is soft. Don't be tempted to look too early or too often, or the heat will be lost and the rice will not cook properly. If you have a rice cooker then this the simplest way to achieve fluffy, perfectly-cooked rice. Note that this recipe applies to long-grain varieties grown on the plains, not the highlands. Also, it will not work for glutinous or short-grain rice. The fluffiness is necessary for Chinese dishes—it is, after all, designed for chopsticks and bowls.

Red bean paste pancakes

Simple to prepare, using a hot water dough to wrap the thin layer of red bean paste, this can be either a dessert or snack. The paste is supposed to be rejuvenating—clarifying the complexion and rounding off an excellent meal all in one go!

300 ml water
300 g plain flour
1 tablespoon lard

200 g can red bean paste
peanut oil

Bring the water to the boil and, in a bowl, add to the flour to make a bread dough. Add the lard just before a smooth dough has formed. Follow method for Chinese Shortcake (page 66), replacing lotus seed paste with red bean paste, but flatten until dough is 1 cm thick.

Pan fry for approximately 3 minutes on each side or until golden brown and crispy.

Composition

 Divide into slices and serve on a plate. They will disappear fast!

Let the Dance Begin

A triumph of elegance and timing seemed to be the prevailing opinion at the Adelaide Hilton on 7 March 1993 for the opening of the new Grange Restaurant.

Appreciative diners commented on the inspired combinations, the sensual progression from dish to dish and sheer quality of each offering. This is a menu for those who enjoy eating well and who look beyond the obvious. Flavour and texture are its hallmarks, and you need only understand the simple Chinese principle of Yin and Yang to fully appreciate why one particular dish is as it is and why it precedes or follows another. It is slightly rich—perhaps too so for younger tastes—and is distinguished by a heightened sense of the order of things and of timing.

This menu is a homage to the power of change. There is a merger of classical influences with contemporary style. Do not concentrate on the individual elements, or the impression could be false. Understanding of the dishes will come through the intelligent combination of presentation, as well as visual appreciation and the actual flavours and textures of the individual components.

Serve the dishes in Chinese banquet style; with the distinctions between early and main courses somewhat blurred. The European penchant for soup at the beginning and the Chinese tradition of soup at either the beginning *or* the end of the banquet are overturned by the appearance of the consommé midway through. There are refreshing moments—the clean acid sweetness of the pickled raw fish; the simple green salad and later the tea sorbet to restore the interest and gird the tastebuds.

When you undertake this menu remember that it relies strongly on the integration of freshness, richness, simple presentation and contrast for its success. If it is well presented, visual appreciation will enhance the flavours. Choose the very best and the freshest ingredients otherwise it will be less successful. Analyse each stage of preparation carefully before you begin and allow time. Above all, strive for a sense of festivity in the presentation and amongst your guests. In that way you will create the harmony the menu deserves.

The night of 7 March 1993 was a premonition of things to come as Cheong became consultant chef at the Grange Restaurant, Hilton International Hotel, Adelaide in March 1995. The restaurant is European in style with a vineyard theme reflecting its South Australian location. This gives a provincial touch to an essentially elegant and comfortable setting. The menu is brimming with exciting taste experiences, from braised possum to crab tea; old favourites like shark lips; and the delectable proposition of saltwater duck and drunken chicken.

The menu is important for another reason—it represents the starting place for this book.

Let the Dance Begin recipes

DEEP-FRIED OYSTERS WITH GARLIC CHIVES
IN BEAN-CURD PASTRY

CHINESE-STYLE PICKLED RAW FISH
WITH STEAMED MUSSELS

VENISON CONSOMMÉ WITH SHARK-FIN POUCH

WARM SALAD OF PIG'S HEAD WITH BABY VEGETABLES

CRISP SPICED PIGEON ON SNOW-PEA SHOOT RISOTTO

RAGOUT OF POSSUM WITH ROOT VEGETABLES

GREEN SALAD

CARAMELISED PEAR NAPOLEON
WITH TEA SORBET

Deep-fried oysters with garlic chives in bean-curd pastry

This dish is reminiscent of a Chinese banquet opener: complete in itself yet holding the promise of what is to come—a light-hearted beginning to a more serious and sumptuous occasion. Being the first dish, it can take full advantage of anticipation and appetite, making it the 'luckiest dish' on the menu. The sea (oyster) meets the earth (chives); sea salt and sweet grass flavours intermingle, harmonious yet contrasting. A little pork, pheasant breast, and scallop, the hint of chives and two centred oysters combine in this hors d'oeuvre. The combination is lightly steamed, coated with egg and flour, then placed in bean-curd pastry and deep-fried. Steaming melts the fat and enriches the flavour of the scallops. A sprinkle of prickly ash over the deep-fried oyster adds aroma, and the deep-frying enhances and seals in the flavours.

Wine: 1987 Croser Sparkling—a celebratory beginning to the evening.

1 large pheasant breast	2 teaspoons sugar
200 g scallops	½ teaspoon white pepper
12 oysters	2 tablespoons tapioca starch
1 teaspoon ginger juice	½ bunch garlic chives, chopped
1 teaspoon rice wine	80 g pork fat, finely chopped
4 sheets bean-curd skin	300 g water chestnuts, chopped
1 whole egg	peanut oil
1 teaspoon sesame oil	prickly ash
1 teaspoon salt	lemon juice

Mince the pheasant breast and chop the scallops finely and chill.

Lightly steam the oysters for one minute then marinate them in the ginger juice and rice wine for 20 minutes. Reserve the liquid.

Cut the bean-curd skin into strips 6 cm x 10 cm, wipe with acidulated water and steam only to moistened stage.

In a mixer on slow speed, mix minced pheasant, scallops, egg, sesame oil, salt, sugar, pepper and tapioca starch. Finish by adding garlic chives, water chestnuts, pork fat and the oyster marinade. Mix to a firm consistency. Take a small amount of the mixture, place two oysters in the centre and roll into a log, approximately 4 cm x 10 cm. Lightly brush with water and wrap in the bean-curd skins. Place the bundles on a tray and steam for 10 minutes and then allow to cool. Heat the peanut oil in a shallow saucepan and deep-fry the bundles until golden brown. Cut into 5 cm lengths and sprinkle with prickly ash and a squeeze of lemon juice.

Composition

 Place a napkin on the serving dish to absorb oil and arrange the pastries on top.

Chinese-style pickled raw fish with steamed mussels

An 'entrée' to the New Year—this is a dish often served between the second and fifteenth day of Chinese New Year, and welcomed by young and old. Traditionally it is stirred by all members of the family so that prosperity for the year is 'stirred' from its sleep to touch all present. Rawness, usually shunned by the Chinese, is here a celebration of freshness, but disguised subtly by the flavour of the 'pickle'. Traditionally the chosen fish is killed, cleaned and sliced just before serving. The fish does not rest in the pickling mixture—the two are combined and eaten at once.

In this case the method is adapted: the 'stirring' is complete and only eating remains to be done. The pickle consists of finely shredded young carrot, daikon, beetroot, and spring onion; coriander and lime leaf add flavour and piquancy; and a sauce of lemon, plum and sorghum-based Chinese rose wine completes the pickle. Toasted sesame seeds, roasted peanuts and light deep-fried pastry are sprinkled on top for instant flavour and effect.

Wine: 1989 Argyle Oregon Riesling—a double sweetness when combined with the fish.

Pickled fish

500 g absolutely fresh fish
 (Atlantic salmon, snapper,
 mei-mei, dolphin fish or whiting)
½ tablespoon salt
½ tablespoon sugar
24 mussels in shell
30 g each carrots, daikon, beetroot,
 green carrots, candied vegetables

5 tablespoons lemon plum sauce
 (see page 220)
½ teaspoon Chinese rose wine
zest of ½ lime
6 stalks coriander
2 tablespoons olive oil

Noodle pastries
plain noodle dough (see page 230)

Garnish

pinch of white pepper
pinch of ground cinnamon
½ tablespoon toasted peanuts,
 finely chopped
1 teaspoon toasted sesame seeds
1 Kaffir lime leaf, finely shredded

5 slices Japanese pickled ginger,
 finely shredded
6 drops sesame oil
1 finely shredded spring onion,
 white only
1 sprig coriander

Pickled fish

Lightly season the raw fish with salt and sugar and chill for 2 hours. Slice very finely. Steam the mussels for 3–4 minutes, enough for the shells to open slightly. Remove the meat and reserve the juices. Chill mussel meat in iced water then return to shells. Finely shred the vegetables. Mix the plum sauce with the raw fish and shredded vegetables and twirl with a fork to form a 5 cm diameter ball. Mix together lime, coriander and olive oil to make a dressing.

Noodle pastries

Make the noodle pastries by rolling the dough out thinly. Cut into diamond shapes 3 cm in length. Deep-fry without colouring the pastry too much.

Composition

Place the fish salad in the centre of the plate and sprinkle with white pepper and ground cinnamon. Place steamed mussels in their shells around the salad. Spoon the dressing over the mussels. Place deep-fried pastries around the fish salad, between the salad and the mussels. Sprinkle over the remaining garnish ingredients.

Venison consommé with shark-fin pouch

A group of French gastronomes visiting Australia expressed their satisfaction with this dish generously and noisily. They understood instinctively that it was a juxtaposition, a Yin–Yang dish offering the heat of game and ginger, with the coolness of the shark's fin in a single surprising bite. It could almost be a metaphor for this land itself: hot, Yang—red centre, earth and marsupial pouch; cool, Yin— an endless coastline, sea and shark.

A rich consommé of venison with sherry is host to the pouch, filled with shark fin and ginger–a vigorous combination of flavours. The pouch is formed with noodle dough, which has a soft but tight texture. Remember to leave enough consommé in your bowl to take a final mouthful after the sherry has been drunk.

Wine: Valdespino Amontillado sherry 'Tio Diego'—sweetish, nutty, creamy, wood flavour; a perfect foil for the consommé.

Farce for clarification
1 kg venison shin
200 g chicken giblets
25 g each finely chopped leeks,
  carrots, tomatoes, mushrooms
fresh thyme, sage, parsley

4 eggwhites
100 ml water
3 litres brown veal stock
  (see page 226), at room
  temperature

Shark-fin soup

4 dried black Chinese mushrooms	1 chicken breast
4 spring onions	3 tablespoons peanut oil
1 tin shark's fin	3 cups white chicken stock
4 tablespoons dry sherry	(see page 224)
3 slices ginger	1 teaspoon salt
4 cups water	2 tablespoons cornflour

Shark-fin pouch

500 g plain noodle dough	1 eggwhite
(see page 230)	
200 g chilled (set)	
Shark-fin Soup (see above)	

Garnish

sprig of tarragon leaves	Valdespino sherry, ½ teaspoon per
	cup of soup

Farce for clarification

Chop the venison meat and giblets very finely. Add leeks, carrots, tomatoes, mushrooms and herbs. Whisk the eggwhites lightly and mix into the venison mixture. Incorporate the water until you have formed a batter. Stir the mixture into the veal stock and slowly bring it to the boil in a saucepan, stirring constantly to prevent the mixture from sticking to the bottom. Reduce heat when it reaches the boil and simmer on a very low heat for 1 hour.

By this stage the consommé should be a clear golden colour. Ladle (do not tip) the consommé carefully through cheesecloth or filter paper. This ensures clarity. Set aside and reheat later.

Shark-fin soup

Soak the dried mushrooms in water for about 30 minutes.

Trim 2 spring onions and add to a pan with the shark's fin, half the sherry, ginger slices and water. Bring to the boil, then simmer, covered, for 15 minutes. Drain the shark's fin and discard the liquid, spring onions and ginger.

Remove the skin from the chicken breast and shred the meat. Shred the soaked mushrooms, and cut the remaining spring onions in 4 cm long pieces.

Heat the oil and brown the spring onion pieces lightly then discard. Add chicken and stir-fry until it loses its pinkness (about 1 minute). Add most of the stock (reserving about 1/4 cup), salt, shark's fin, mushrooms and the remaining sherry. Bring to the boil then simmer, covered, for about 30 minutes.

Blend the cornflour and remaining stock, then stir into the soup until it thickens. Chill until it sets.

Shark-fin pouch

Roll the dough out very thinly and cut six 7 cm diameter rounds. Divide the chilled shark-fin soup into 6 equal portions. Form into quenelles (the shape of a dessertspoon). Place in the centre of each noodle pastry and lightly brush the edges of the pastry with the eggwhite. Seal the edges to form a pouch. Brush a plate with oil. Place the dumplings on the plate and steam for 10 minutes.

Composition

Place each steamed dumpling into a soup cup with a few tarragon leaves then ladle the consommé into the cup until it covers about three-quarters of the dumpling. Add half a teaspoon of sherry per cup and serve hot.

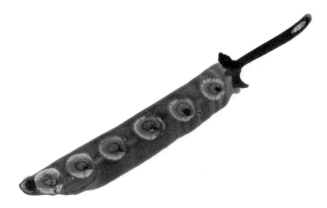

Warm salad of pig's head with baby vegetables

This dish was inspired by Joël Robuchon, of the Parisian restaurant Jamin. The pig's head is a challenge. Essentially crude, it is transformed into an elegant dish in which texture, nutrition, flavour, and colour are paraded and savoured; an exercise in harmony and balance. For those who enjoy texture, an element of great importance in Asian cuisine, this dish offers a crunchy, velvety, gelatinous, dense, crisp, smooth and bountiful gift.

The pig's head is cooked Chinese village style, with garlic and salted mustard greens. A piece from each part of the head is served on each plate: the cheek, snout, brain, tongue and ear. These meats are accompanied by the youngest and crispest of baby vegetables and finished with a sauce composed of rich veal glaze with tomato, Madeira, and a hint of ginger. The salted mustard greens combined with the garlic and master stock impart a rich deep flavour which meets and mingles with the sweetness of the pork, creating a seductive aroma. This is, truly speaking, a restaurant dish. There are four cooking stages, each with their own sets of ingredients. The preparation of the pig's head should be started 24 hours in advance.

Wine: 1988 Hugel Gerwurztraminer 'Reserve Personelle'—fruitiness to offset the richness of the dish.

Steeping stock

225 g preserved vegetables
salted mustard greens
5 whole garlic cloves
2 cinnamon sticks
2 whole star anise
175 ml dark soy sauce

175 ml light soy sauce
1 tablespoon white peppercorns
3 tablespoons rice wine
½ teaspoon cloves
2½ tablespoons salt

Pig's head

2 pig's heads, halved
  (ask your butcher)
3 tablespoons salt
200 g rock sugar

vinegar or lemon juice
butter
freshly ground black pepper

Sauce

500 ml chicken jus
  (see page 224)
500 ml veal jus
  (see page 226)
3 tablespoons ginger juice

1–1½ cups fresh tomato purée
  (see page 221)
3 tablespoons Madeira
1 teaspoon freshly ground
  white peppercorns

Vegetables

18 whole baby turnips
18 baby carrots
18 small snow peas
1 kg young broad beans

12 shiitake mushrooms, small
6 young garlic shoots
2 cloves garlic

Steeping stock

Put all ingredients in a deep stockpot with 7 litres of water and simmer
for 45 minutes.

Pig's head

Remove the brain from each head and clean off all blood and membrane.
Place the brains in iced water for 1 hour. Remove tongues and ears (they
will come away easily when pulled) and blanch these in boiling water, then
refresh in iced water. Rub salt into each head then soak in iced water
overnight. The next day, blanch the heads then refresh in iced water.
Steep in stock for 1 hour. Add the rock sugar after 30 minutes.

Brain: Blanch in boiling water with a little vinegar or lemon juice. Sauté in butter, season with pepper, then remove from the pan and place on absorbent paper.

Tongue and ears: Tie the blanched ears in muslin cloth, simmer in some of the stock and remove when tender. Bind the blanched tongues together with string and simmer until tender (make sure it is not over-cooked). Remove the outer skin.

Head: Remove the skin from the head, retaining the snout. Carefully remove the cheek meat as well as meat from the inside of the ears and divide into 6 pieces. Reheat very gently in the steeping stock, thus ensuring the meat remains moist.

Cut the pig's ears into thin strips, pig's tongue into thin slices, pig's snout into thin slices and pig's brain into six pieces.

Sauce

Prepare this as the pig's head is simmering in the stock.

Combine chicken and veal jus and reduce to one-third to achieve the right consistency. Add ginger juice and tomato purée to taste. Finish by adding Madeira and pepper. Set aside and reheat at the composition stage.

Vegetables

Peel and clean turnips and carrots. Halve the turnips. Blanch each type of vegetable separately. String the snow peas. Blanch the broad beans then peel until you get to the tender inner bean. Halve the shiitake mush-rooms. Clean the garlic shoots; peel and crush the garlic finely. Just before composition, gently heat the vegetables by sautéing in butter with the garlic and garlic shoots for 2 minutes.

Composition

Arrange brain, cheek, snout and tongue portions in the centre of the plate and place the warm sautéed baby vegetables on top. Pour sauce over these, sprinkle pig's ears over the dish and moisten with more sauce.

Crisp spiced pigeon on snow-pea shoot risotto

Six-week-old pigeons or squabs, the stars of this dish, are on the threshold of flight, fine feathered and beginning to eat grain independently. In this main course they are tender yet crisp, interestingly spiced, without distraction. The snow-pea shoots and bland risotto are but extras on the stage.

King or Carneau pigeons are best. A twelve-hour marinade rub of toasted sea salt, herbs and spices imparts aroma. Tim Pak Poy developed this rub for a special dinner at Claude's in Sydney. The intrusion of Sichuan peppercorns transforms the taste to something unexpected yet familiar. After blanching, the pigeon is deep-fried twice then allowed to rest before being boned and served on a bed of snow-pea shoot risotto. The anointing sauce is overlaid with aged balsamic vinegar to counteract the pigeon's fattiness and to enhance its flavour. Begin preparation a day in advance and discover the master chef within yourself.

Wine: 1988 Prunotto Nebbiolo d'Alba 'Oschetti'—a soft red offering flavour and fruit without sacrificing lightness.

Pigeon rub
2½ tablespoons sea salt
6 whole juniper berries
¼ stick cinnamon
½ fresh bay leaf
sprig fresh thyme

sprig fresh sage
1 teaspoon Sichuan peppercorns,
   crushed
2 cloves
6 female squab

To cook the pigeon

2 litres white chicken stock
  (see page 224)
100 g maltose

300 ml malt vinegar
peanut oil

Sauce

pigeon wings, liver, giblets,
  feet and carcasses (as above)
peanut or olive oil
300 g mirepoix

1 litre brown chicken stock
  (see page 223)
1 cup Prunotto wine (Italian brand)

Risotto

100 g butter
300 ml chicken fumet
  (see page 225)
½ teaspoon lemon zest
200 g Arborio rice

stock from sauce above
salt
freshly ground black pepper
3 tablespoons snow-pea shoots
aged balsamic vinegar

Pigeon rub

Sprinkle sea salt over a metal tray and place in oven at 180°C for
15 minutes. Combine salt, herbs and spices and grind finely. Rub this
marinade over the pigeons and leave for 12 hours.

To cook the pigeon

Heat the chicken stock to a simmer. Blanch the pigeons in 2 litres of
simmering water for twenty seconds, then refresh in cold water. Transfer
the pigeons to the hot white chicken stock and steep for 10 minutes.
The stock temperature should be under 90°C—don't let it boil. Remove
pigeons and brush with a mixture of maltose and vinegar and hang up to
dry in the fridge or in front of a fan for at least 10 hours.

Heat the peanut oil and deep-fry the pigeons for 2 minutes, to skin-deep
stage only; allow to rest for 3 minutes. Deep-fry for a further 5 minutes.
Allow the pigeon to rest for 20 minutes then bone. Remove the breast and
legs. Remove the thigh bones. Keep the breast and legs aside, and use the
rest in the sauce.

Sauce

Chop pigeon parts into small pieces. Heat some oil in a frying-pan and brown the pigeon and vegetables. Add stock and simmer for 2 hours. Strain and skim off any fat. Take half the quantity of stock and reduce to one-third (set aside the other half for the risotto), and add in the wine.

Risotto

Grease a baking tray well with some of the butter. In a saucepan, bring the chicken fumet to the boil and add in lemon zest and rice, cooking gently until the liquid has been absorbed. Do not cover with a lid. Spread the rice over the tray and place in the refrigerator immediately to arrest the cooking process. (This ensures that the rice will not be overcooked when it is reheated.) When cool, reheat risotto in the stock until all the liquid has been absorbed. Mound the remaining butter into the risotto for creaminess and add seasonings. At the very last stage, add the snow-pea shoots.

Composition

 Place the snow-pea risotto on each plate and a pigeon breast and legs on top. Spoon sauce over the pigeon to moisten it, then sprinkle with aged balsamic vinegar.

Ragout of possum with root vegetables

*For those who are feeling nervous about possum-eating I can only say
that for me it is no different to consuming goat, venison, hare or any
other Australian game meat. I don't hesitate therefore to prepare it
in the European style, as one would prepare traditional game. My
preference, however, is to cook it with the de-furred skin left on—
Asian style—to increase the game flavour. John Ho says possum tastes
just like flying fox; others expect it to taste like hung English game,
but it doesn't really have the same intensity.*

When Cheong put possum on the menu at the Adelaide Hilton in 1995, it
hit the headlines. Australians were still getting used to the idea of eating
kangaroo, but a Cantonese business delegation had, so the story goes,
prompted a Tasmanian farmer to switch from growing apples to farming
possums for export to China. Possum is reared for consumption in
Tasmania only, where the animal is almost in plague proportions; in all
other Australian states it is protected, so meat should be purchased from
licensed producers only.

Ragout of possum
2 whole possums, about 2 kg each
  with skin on
1½ stalks celery
3 medium carrots
2 whole onions
2 cloves garlic
5 parsley stalks
2 bay leaves
2.5 litres red wine

60 g clarified butter
120 ml brandy
4 ripe tomatoes
60 g mushrooms
1.5 litres brown chicken stock
  (see page 223)
240 ml port
100 ml ginger juice

Root vegetables
300 g bacon lardon
18 small pickling onions
250 g mushrooms
18 small baby carrots

18 baby turnips
6 slices thin white bread
extra clarified butter
18 snow peas

Garnish
4 basil leaves, finely sliced

Ragout of possum

Clean the possums, discarding the innards but retaining the liver and hearts, and remove the legs. Separate the rib cage from the loin and divide the loin into four pieces.

Roughly dice the celery, carrots, onions and garlic and place in a large bowl with the loin and legs of possum. Add the parsley stalks and bay leaves and cover with red wine. Marinate for 24 hours.

Remove the possum pieces and dry them on kitchen paper. Strain the vegetables, reserving the marinade.

Heat the butter and sauté the possum pieces until brown all over. Flame the possum pieces with brandy then remove them from the pan. Add the marinated vegetables to the same pan and brown them slightly. Add the innards, hearts, mushrooms and tomatoes, and continue to cook until all juices have evaporated. Add in the red wine marinade and chicken stock and bring to the boil then strain it through a fine sieve and return it to the vegetables. Finally, add in the possum pieces, cover with foil and cook in the oven at 160°C for 3 hours.

Remove the possum pieces, cover and keep warm. Strain the cooking liquid into a saucepan and reduce, skimming off any excess fat. Add the port and ginger juice and cook until it forms a glaze.

Root vegetables

Remove the rind from the bacon and cut into 5 mm strips. Peel the onions, quarter the mushrooms, and cut the baby carrots and turnips into small pieces. Cut 6 heart-shaped croutons out of the bread and toast in clarified butter until golden. Blanch the bacon, then fry until light brown. Remove it from the pan and add the onions, mushroom, carrot and turnip. Cook in the oven for about 5 minutes until soft. Blanch the snow peas.

Composition

Arrange one loin and leg on a plate and cover with a little sauce. Sprinkle the onions, mushrooms and bacon over the possum. Arrange the carrots, turnips and snow peas around the possum, with a crouton on top. Sprinkle over the basil chiffonnade.

Green salad

There is no mystery in this salad. It offers a moment to pause, cleanse and refresh the palate before the dessert appears. A combination of Asian and European greens, it features a simple Jo Grilli olive oil and vinegar dressing, and a crispy garnish.

Jo Grilli (or any good quality)
  olive oil
champagne vinegar
salt
freshly ground black pepper

frisée lettuce
lamb's lettuce
sat choy
mitsuma

Garnish
1 tablespoon roasted pinenuts
1 tablespoon crisp bacon pieces

freshly ground black pepper

Put olive oil and vinegar in a mixing bowl and add salt and pepper. Toss in the salad leaves and marinate for 1 minute.

Composition

Place a small amount of salad on each side plate and sprinkle with garnish ingredients, finishing with the freshly ground pepper.

Caramelised pear napoleon with tea sorbet

A classic torte dessert best timed for the arrival of new season pears and complemented by a contemporary, clean, cold tea sorbet. This dessert looks like an elegant classic and behaves like one, until you move from the napoleon to the sorbet. The contrast is arresting. At this point in the banquet the appetite must be cajoled. The tea is an interruption; it grabs our attention, breaking through the creamy sweetness of the wine and the smooth crème. Thus it is the tea sorbet, rather than the pear coulis or the rich crème and crisp inviting pastry that seduces the palate. The contrast between light–clean and rich–creamy expresses the Yin–Yang principle once again. A triumph of flakiness and lightness, the pastry holds together to the last, breaking cleanly as you bite it.

The six stages in this dessert demand skill and patience, especially for the home cook who doesn't have the advantages of a restaurant kitchen. Nevertheless, the results will justify the effort.

The torte is layered with crème pâtisserie and lightened with Italian meringue. The refreshing tea sorbet is spiced with pear eau de vie, and the pear is caramelised in a syrup of vanilla spiced with anise.

Wine: 1985 Petaluma Botrytis 'Essence'—a rich sweet white wine.

Vanilla anise syrup
300 ml water
125 g granulated sugar

1 vanilla pod, seeded (retain seeds)
4 whole star anise

Pastry cream
1 vanilla pod, seeded (retain seeds)
1 cup milk
2 large egg yolks
4 tablespoons granulated sugar

1 tablespoon flour
1 tablespoon cornflour
1½ tablespoons Italian meringue
(use less if the mixture is moist)

Pear coulis
1 pear, peeled, cored and cubed
125 ml stock syrup
  (see page 232)

1 vanilla pod, seeded
4 tablespoons lemon juice
1 tablespoon pear eau de vie

Tea sorbet
300 ml spring water
3 teaspoons lychee tea
300 g sugar

juice of ½ lemon
2 eggwhites
pear eau de vie

Pastry
500 g puff pastry
  (see page 230)

pure icing sugar

Caramelised pears
6 Duchess pears
100 g clarified butter

pear eau de vie
300 ml vanilla anise syrup (above)

Vanilla anise syrup

Mix water and sugar and bring to the boil. Remove from the heat then infuse with the vanilla seeds and star anise.

Pastry cream

Combine vanilla seeds with the milk and bring to the boil. Set aside. Whisk egg yolks and sugar until light and pale. Fold in flour and cornflour. Pour hot milk onto the egg mixture, incorporate, and return to the heat until it thickens. Cool the mixture. When cold, incorporate enough Italian meringue into the mixture to lighten it.

Pear coulis

Cook the pear in some stock syrup and add in the vanilla pod and lemon juice and cook until soft. Remove the pod. Purée then add the eau de vie.

Tea sorbet

Bring one-third of the spring water to the boil and brew the lychee tea in it for 10 minutes then strain. Boil the remaining water with the sugar, add to the tea and allow to cool. Add the lemon juice. Whip the eggwhites lightly and add to the sorbet mixture, then freeze. Add a teaspoon of pear eau de vie per serving of the finished sorbet just before serving.

Pastry

Preheat the oven to 210°C. Roll out two sheets of pastry to a 10 cm x 18 cm rectangle 2 mm thick. Dot with a fork and weigh it down with another tray to prevent it rising. Chill the pastry before baking in the oven. Cook until pale golden in colour. Cut into 4 cm x 6 cm rectangles. Dust with icing sugar and caramelise under the griller.

Caramelised pears

Peel and core pears and cut into halves. Sauté them in the butter. Remove pears and deglaze the pan with pear eau de vie and vanilla anise syrup until thick. Return pears to the pan, cover with syrup and cook for a few more minutes.

Composition

Arrange one rectangle of pastry on each plate and cover with a layer of crème pâtisserie and the halves of caramelised pear. Then place another layer of pastry on top. Dust with icing sugar. Pour pear coulis around the pears. Position the sorbet to one side.

Adelaide Extravaganza

T his is the last menu chapter—the right moment to talk about the way Cheong's approach to cooking has developed…

Remember the shop house in High Street, now Jalan Bandar? When I was nine and living there my uncle gave me a reject dressed spring chicken with a broken leg which I was supposed to throw away. I decided not to waste it. After seasoning it with salt and soy sauce and starting a fire to heat up oil in a wok, I deep-fried the bird until it was crisp. My uncle was dumbfounded that I had cooked it and was pleased to share it with me! From that time on I was interested in food and its preparation without having any sense that this would ultimately be my profession. I used to cook for my family and friends and I did so without being told exactly how to do it. I decided on the amounts, the ingredients and I kept tasting and adjusting and striving to achieve the correct taste and appearance. So I got used to being my own judge. My culture also demanded the freshest of ingredients—an essential aspect of my approach—and I knew how to recognise quality produce. I always sought density of flavour and contrasting textures in my dishes. For density try Sichuan peppercorns and Indian black cardamom. For textural contrast, try sea cucumber or deep-fried shrimp. These are illuminating ingredients, and if you are ready to explore Australian cuisine at its best you will welcome this challenge.

When I left Malaysia to come to Australia, I brought considerable cooking knowledge absorbed during my life there. From the start of Neddy's I knew that the time had come to move on from that culture and to develop a new style. I had by then been exposed to other genres as a chef—Australian pubs, Greek, Indian, French, Italian and Spanish. I was also aware that Australia was a frontier for ideas—its lack of strong food traditions, its diversity of cultures, and its casual style favoured individual expression. People were moving well beyond the pedestrian overcooked fare of former times—they wanted flavoursome, carefully cooked dishes; no more dried-out roasts and grey fish. Taste, look and aroma were in demand.

I read cookbooks avidly at this time, adding to my repertoire as I went. Most of my dishes have evolved from my own interpretation of particular styles—I have never slavishly followed either traditions or others' prescriptions. I aim for good finish, flavour and quality of cooking; as long as I achieve these, I am unconcerned about departing from traditional method or combining unusual ingredients.

Moving from running a restaurant to becoming a lecturer at the Regency Hotel School has not deterred me from this path. My students have responded very positively to my unorthodox style—occasionally to the horror of my formally trained colleagues—but I have also learnt from them. My desserts especially have benefited from exposure to traditional dessert chefs—Swiss, English, German and French. I am creating a more haute-cuisine style with my own signature. Being more professional has not constrained my interest in originality.

Whenever I start thinking of a dish I immediately consider the setting. How will a person feel about this dish in a particular setting? I try to think about the whole experience of the diner, not just the dish itself. I will envisage the taste and presentation of the dish down to the smallest point before I start. Also, if I am going to cook something from a certain part of the world, I like it to reflect a sense of place— the landscape, the colours, the people, the art.

We are embracing diversity in Australia. I like to capture it on the plate.

Adelaide Extravaganza recipes

DRUNKEN CHICKEN, JELLYFISH SALAD, 'SMOKED' FISH
AND BLACK-PEPPERED PINEAPPLE

SLOW-BRAISED ABALONE, VEAL SWEETBREADS
AND BLACK MOSS

RED-ROAST SNAPPER WITH SHAVED CUTTLEFISH
AND LEEK FONDUE

LOIN OF LAMB WITH SHAHJIRA SPICE AND ALMOND CRUST
AND BLACK CARDAMOM-SCENTED JUS

PORK HOCK WITH WOOD FUNGUS

STEAMED BOUILLABAISSE CUSTARD IN SAFFRON FISH CONSOMMÉ
WITH FENNEL PURÉE

VEAL CUTLET WITH SHRIMP AND GREEN TEA

SALTWATER DUCK ON CHINESE CABBAGE
WITH WATERCRESS SAUCE

VACHERIN GÂTEAU WITH MANGO SORBET AND FROMAGE BLANC SORBET,
SERVED WITH WARM CHOCOLATE TART

ICED FRUIT SOUP WITH HOT GINGER DATE PUDDING
AND COCONUT SORBET

MARJOLAINE

Drunken chicken, jellyfish salad, 'smoked' fish and black-peppered pineapple

'Foong mei' translates, with some difficulty, into 'the aromatic wind of the region'. Aromatic is not meant to imply only the scent of the region but all of its characteristics—colours, customs, language, people, food. This dish is an Australian foong mei—it has Asian connotations but it has been transformed by its Adelaide setting.

Reminiscent of Mediterranean meze or antipasto, this dish is designed to be served as an appetiser. It displays subtle flavours, muted colours and great variety in textures and form. The Dijon dressing adds a gentle piquancy and marks the move from Asia to Australia. Black-peppered pineapple with vanilla is the surprise—the vanilla takes away the pineapple's sharpness and makes it silky, while the pepper adds spiciness. The 'smoked' fish is actually deep fried. The deep frying and glazing, combined with the sesame oil, gives it a smoky flavour.

Marinade

2 tablespoons stock syrup
  (see page 232)
1 tablespoon gin
½ tablespoon sesame oil
½ tablespoon ginger juice
½ tablespoon spring onion juice

1 tablespoon sake
  (or Chinese brown rice wine)
2 tablespoons white chicken stock
  (see page 224)
1 teaspoon fish sauce

Drunken chicken

1 whole chicken
1 tablespoon salt

7 litres white chicken stock
  (see page 224)

Seasoning

1 tablespoon light soy sauce
1 teaspoon spring onion juice

½ tablespoon sake
  (or Chinese yellow rice wine)

Jellyfish salad

250 g jellyfish
2 cm knob ginger, finely shredded
1 bunch coriander, leaves
  and stems

1 fresh chilli, finely shredded
salt
freshly ground black pepper
1 teaspoon sesame oil

Chinese 'smoked' fish

500 g fish (trevally, bream or snook)
20 ml rice wine
½ teaspoon five spice powder
1 tablespoon light soy sauce
3 spring onions, white only,
  cut into sticks
1 cm knob ginger, sliced
100 ml white chicken stock
  (see page 224)

2½ tablespoons dark soy sauce
1 tablespoon crushed rock sugar
1 whole star anise
3 pieces dried tangerine peel
500 ml peanut oil
1 teaspoon sesame oil
1 teaspoon spring onion paste

Black-peppered pineapple

½ pineapple, peeled
1 vanilla pod, seeds only

1 teaspoon freshly ground black
  pepper

Dijon mustard dressing

1 tablespoon Dijon mustard
juice of ½ lemon
2 tablespoons crème fraîche

1 tablespoon chardonnay
2 drops Tabasco
½ tablespoon grapeseed oil

Garnish

300 g stringless beans, blanched
  until tender

Marinade

Combine all ingredients.

Drunken chicken

Use the cooking method in Perfect Steeped White Chicken in Simple
Chinese Home Menu. Allow the chicken to steep in the stock until cold,
then plunge into iced water to chill. Dry the chicken cavity *thoroughly* so
that the chicken will retain its freshness and firm texture while marinating.
Hang it up to dry.

Bone and slice the chicken and arrange on a serving dish then pour over
the marinade and allow the chicken to stand for 30 minutes.

Seasoning

Combine all ingredients and drizzle over chicken.

Jellyfish salad

Soak jellyfish in cold water for a few hours, changing the water frequently. Rinse the jellyfish then drain the water until the jellyfish is very dry. Shred the jellyfish finely and add ginger, coriander and chilli. Season with salt, pepper and sesame oil.

Chinese 'smoked' fish

Cut the fish into pieces. Mix together the rice wine, five spice powder, light soy sauce, half the spring onion sticks and half the ginger, and marinate the fish pieces for 20 minutes. In a saucepan heat stock, dark soy sauce, sugar, star anise, tangerine peel and remaining ginger and spring onion. Simmer until it turns to a glaze then strain. Remove fish pieces from marinade and pat dry with kitchen paper or a cloth. Heat peanut oil in a frying-pan, deep-fry fish once in moderate heat and then remove. Fry it again in the same oil, heated to smoking point. Fry until crispy then mix it with the glaze. Heat sesame oil, add spring onion paste and fry until fragrant then mix it with the fish.

Black-peppered pineapple

Cut the pineapple into quarters. Remove the hard centre stem and slice into 1 cm thick slices and combine with the vanilla seeds and black pepper.

Dijon mustard dressing

Combine dressing ingredients.

Composition

Trim the stringless beans into equal lengths. Place four or five beans on each plate and dress with a teaspoon of dressing. Place drunken chicken on the top. On the side arrange a tablespoon of jellyfish salad. Arrange smoked fish and then the pineapple to complete a circle on the plate.

Slow-braised abalone, veal sweetbreads and black moss

When we first served green-lipped abalone at Neddy's it was around $20 per kilo; now it is $200 per kilo, a local disadvantage of international popularity. In my opinion it is still worth it—the black-lipped variety is not as thick and cannot withstand long cooking without becoming rubbery. Choose the green variety if you can get it. The Cantonese dish is called abalone with black moss and is usually served at Chinese New Year. Two cooking methods are used here— slow braising and thin slicing then, in the last seconds, warming through. I say seconds because a minute would be too long. The thin slices are used as a garnish on top of the slow-braised abalone. The daring combination of black moss, oyster sauce, butter and finely sliced basil appeals to me. To then add pine mushrooms and veal sweetbreads is a brave flourish, but the result is stunning.

The South Australian green-lipped abalone, in huge demand in Asia, is sweet and tender, as long as it is not overcooked. This dish is derived from a very traditional Cantonese dish, combined with a French-style offal dish. The sweet tastes mingle but the textures contrast.

Abalone and sweetbreads

400 g fresh green-lipped abalone
1 cup peanut oil
2 slices fresh ginger
1 spring onion
200 ml brown chicken stock
  (see page 223)

150 g veal sweetbreads
juice of ½ lemon
2 tablespoons butter
1 Chinese lettuce (or cos)
salt
freshly ground black pepper

Sauce

½ tablespoon peanut oil
1 teaspoon shallots, finely chopped
1 tablespoon ginger juice
80 g pine mushrooms
20 g black moss
3 tablespoons chardonnay

1½ tablespoons oyster sauce
¼ teaspoon dried scallop paste
brioche (see page 229)
6 basil leaves, finely sliced
2 cubes unsalted butter

Abalone and sweetbreads

Pry three-quarters of the abalone muscles from the shells, and remove and discard the stomachs. Scrub with a hard brush to remove all the green from the shells. Blanch abalone quickly in hot peanut oil to seal then wash in warm water. (Reserve a tablespoon of the oil for later use.) Add ginger slices and spring onion to the chicken stock and cook the abalone at a very low heat for 1½ hours. Cool in the stock. Remove abalone (reserving stock for later use) and slice.

Thirty minutes before serving, lightly freeze the remaining fresh abalone, then slice very thinly and set aside for use in the sauce.

Blanch the sweetbreads in acidulated water. Refresh in cold water and peel off membranes and fat. Heat the butter, add sweetbreads and brown on both sides. Place in the oven for 5 minutes at 160°C, turning halfway through. Cut into thin slices.

Scald the lettuce very quickly in the reserved abalone oil, season with salt and pepper, simmer in 3–4 tablespoons of the reserved chicken stock for 1 minute, then set aside ready for use.

Sauce

Heat oil and add shallot and ginger juice. Add pine mushrooms and black moss, chardonnay, oyster sauce and chicken and abalone stock. Add dried scallop paste. Reduce. Warm through just before serving.

Drop thinly sliced fresh abalone, basil and cubes of unsalted butter into the warm sauce. Whisk lightly for a few seconds

Cut 6 slices of brioche, 1.5 cm thick and 4 cm x 6 cm square. Brush with butter and toast.

Composition

Put brioche in the centre of the plate. Place a bundle of lettuce on the brioche. Place slow-braised abalone slices—about 4—on the lettuce. Arrange sweetbreads around the abalone. Place the thinly sliced warm abalone from the sauce on top of the braised abalone, spooning a small amount of sauce over the top. Arrange the pine mushrooms and black moss next to the sweetbreads. Spoon remaining sauce around the sweetbreads.

Red-roast snapper with shaved cuttlefish and leek fondue

This is an intense dish both for the chef to prepare and for the diner to enjoy. The outer skin of the fish is very distinctly caramel in flavour but inside there is a soft and delicate meat. I call this exciting eating —it combines the Oriental method of preparing fish with French provincial earthiness. It can be garnished with very quickly sautéed snow-pea shoots.

This roast is very slightly braised with the sauce, exuding a delicate flavour. The leek fondue goes well with the flavour and texture of the snapper, and the green sauce brings together the separate elements of the dish. The cuttlefish shavings add another dimension.

Fish
approximately 1.2 kg snapper
fillets (if whole, 1.8–2.2 kg)

60 ml peanut oil

Marinade
1 finely sliced spring onion
3 cm knob ginger, finely sliced
1 tablespoon peanut oil
1 tablespoon light soy sauce
1 tablespoon dark soy sauce

2 tablespoons rice wine
1 teaspoon sugar
salt
freshly ground black pepper

Sauce
2 green chillies
1 tablespoon chopped coriander
    leaves and roots
2 tablespoons chopped celery
    leaves
2 tablespoons chopped spring
    onion greens
1 tablespoon peanut oil
1 teaspoon sesame oil
1 clove chopped garlic

½ tablespoon chopped ginger
1 tablespoon brown bean paste
1½ tablespoons sugar
½ tablespoon rice wine
2½ tablespoons fish stock
    (see page 221)
1 tablespoon oyster sauce
½ tablespoon ginger juice
4 x 1 cm cubes chilled
    unsalted butter

Leek fondue

80 g butter
1 bunch leeks, whites only,
  finely sliced
3 tablespoons white wine
  (Noilly Prat)

100 ml crème fraîche
salt
freshly ground white pepper

Cuttlefish shavings

1 cuttlefish, cleaned and gutted
1 tablespoon peanut oil
1 slice ginger

salt
freshly ground black pepper

Fish

For whole fish, remove the head, gills, guts and scales, then fillet and remove all bones.

Marinade

Combine all marinade ingredients. Marinate fish for 30 minutes.

Remove from marinade, pat dry and shallow-fry with a little oil, skin-side down, until brown and crisp. Turn over, cook for 1 minute then remove.

Sauce

Blend or pound the chillies, coriander, celery leaves and spring onion greens into a green paste. Heat peanut oil and sesame oil, add garlic, ginger and brown bean paste. Add in sugar, then rice wine. Then add green paste and sauté gently for 2 minutes. Strain mixture through a fine sieve and push as much of the paste through as possible with the back of a spoon. Return the green jus to the heat and add fish stock, oyster sauce and ginger juice and reduce to one-third.

Leek fondue

In a pan heat up 20 g of butter and toss in the leeks. Stir for a few minutes then add white wine. Add in the crème fraîche. Reduce to thicken, then add remaining butter. Slowly cook for about 20 minutes until the leek is very tender. Season with salt and pepper.

Cuttlefish shavings

Cut the cuttlefish into halves, lengthwise, then thinly slice from the inside at an angle. Marinate in half the oil and some salt. Heat the remaining oil in a pan with the slice of ginger and, with a shake of the pan, instantly sauté and separate the cuttlefish slices if they stick together. Season with salt and pepper.

Composition

Spread one generous tablespoon of leek fondue onto the centre of the plate. Place the red-roast snapper on top of the fondue. Warm the sauce through and add knobs of unsalted butter whisking to incorporate. Pour around the leek fondue, placing a tablespoon on top of the snapper. Garnish with the cuttlefish shavings.

Loin of lamb with shahjira spice and almond crust and black cardamom-scented jus

Mystical and even erotic, this dish conjures up images of India, and its fascinating spices. When I decided to do this dish I went to the Asian Bazaar in the market and talked to the proprietor, Gihar, about a spice for my lamb crust. I told him that I wanted to know about some spice combinations, but I did not say that I would be using them together, as I eventually did. He introduced me to these two wonderful mixtures. One is puchan puran—consisting of cumin, fenugreek, cardamom, fennel and mustard seeds—a spice generally used for Indian vegetable cooking; the other spice was shahjira, reminiscent of cumin and caraway. I lightened the spice with almond meal. The black cardamom-scented jus has a smoky eucalyptus-like flavour.

As an accompaniment I serve eggplant cooked mughlai style.

Good quality lamb is essential for this dish: South Australia's Kangaroo Island lamb has a salty quality similar to the famous French pré-salé (salt field) lamb. Milk-fed lamb has a very delicate texture and light colour. Cheong considers it the very best eating lamb in Australia—if you can get it. The meat industry is beginning to respond to demand for quality, but regional distinctions are a novelty for Australia.

Lamb

2 milk-fed lamb loins
1½ tablespoons black salt
2 tablespoons olive oil
1½ tablespoons butter, softened
4 tomatoes, peeled, seeded
  and cut into cubes
red wine for deglazing
800 ml brown lamb stock
  (see page 227)

2 black cardamom pods
100 g almond meal
  (purchased ready-made)
15 g shahjira (cumin and caraway)
15 g puchan puran (cumin,
  fenugreek, cardamom, fennel
  and mustard seeds)
2 teaspoons Dijon mustard
extra melted butter

Almond and garlic croquettes

10 hard-boiled eggs
8 cloves garlic, whole
2 tablespoons butter, softened
5 fresh basil leaves, sliced
1 beaten egg

½ cup almond meal
peanut oil
salt
freshly ground black pepper

Eggplant garnish

3 green chillies, whole
salt to taste
150 ml yoghurt
3 eggplants, sliced and salted
2 tablespoons olive oil
½ teaspoon cumin seeds
½ teaspoon mustard seeds

½ teaspoon poppy seeds
6 whole shallots, finely chopped
1 tomato, peeled, seeded, diced
½ teaspoon fresh turmeric
1 teaspoon chopped ginger
1 teaspoon chopped garlic
mint leaves

Lamb

Preheat the oven to 140°C. Trim the sinew from the lamb, leaving the fat on the loin. Keep the trimmings. Season with black salt. Heat the olive oil in an ovenproof pan on top of the stove and seal the lamb well on each side. Place the lamb on a rack and put the rack back in the pan. Brush soft butter over the lamb and cook in the oven for 30 minutes. Baste with juice every 5–10 minutes. Remove from the oven and leave to rest for 30 minutes. Remove all fat and sinew and set the loins aside in a warm place.

Add the raw trimmings and half the tomato to the original pan and fry until there is very little juice remaining.

Deglaze the pan with red wine, then add stock. Reduce to a light glaze consistency, then strain and steep cardamom in the sauce. Mix together almond meal and spice mixtures. Brush loins with mustard and dust with the spiced almond mixture. Pat it down slightly, brush with melted butter and grill under griller. Add remaining tomato cubes to the sauce just before serving.

Almond and garlic croquettes

Force the whole boiled eggs through a sieve to break them up finely. Blanch garlic in boiling water three times, changing water each time. Peel and purée. Add soft butter and basil to the garlic. Add sieved eggs to the mixture, form into cone shapes then freeze until firm. Roll the croquettes in beaten egg and then the almond meal. Fry until golden and sprinkle with salt and pepper.

Eggplant garnish

Lightly salt the whole green chillies and set aside for 20 minutes then add to the yoghurt. Dry, peel and cut the salted eggplant into strips. Heat up oil, add cumin seeds, mustard seeds and poppy seeds. When seeds start to pop, add shallots, tomato, turmeric, ginger, garlic and cook until the oil separates. Add eggplant and cook until tender. Add in chilli and yoghurt mixture.

Composition

For a restaurant touch use a 5 cm diameter pastry cutter to mould eggplant in the centre of individual plates or simply spoon it into the centre. Slice the loin of lamb and arrange five or six slices around the eggplant mixture. Pour sauce around the slices of lamb and garnish with 3 croquettes. Top with mint leaves.

Pork hock with wood fungus

*My dad and I love pork rump—the gelatinous skin and velvety meat.
For today's generation it is important to note that the amount of fat is
reduced by boiling. After marinating the meat is deep-fried until
crispy, then braised. Paradoxically, the deep-frying process further
reduces the fattiness of the meat by releasing the fat into the oil. Rich
sauce and light meat make this a tantalising dish. I added wood
fungus to this dish in honour of a faithful American customer who
tried wood fungus at Neddy's and never forgot it.*

This ancient Chinese dish uses a sauce combination which is supposed to
have been a royal favourite. It has a lot of 'bigness'—rich tahini, brown
bean, hoi sin sauce—a great dish. In Southern China this sauce is used for
a variety of game dishes, and is known as hunter-style sauce (in French 'de
chasseur' and in Italian 'cacciatore'). Serving this dish with Chinese greens
and shallow-fried potatoes works well. Alternatively, try a simple cleansing
salad.

Pork hock

100 g wood fungus
4 pork hocks, deboned
  (ask your butcher to do this)
1 tablespoon salt
1 spring onion
2 slices fresh ginger
2 tablespoons dark soy sauce
1 tablespoon ginger juice
1 tablespoon spring onion juice
500 ml peanut oil
2 tablespoons sesame oil
2 tablespoons extra peanut oil
1 star anise
4 spring onions, chopped

3 cloves garlic, finely chopped
4 cm knob ginger, finely chopped
4 tablespoons tahini
2 tablespoons red bean curd
3 tablespoons brown bean paste
2 tablespoons light soy sauce
60 ml rice wine
1 tablespoon vinegar chilli sauce
  (or chilli sauce)
2 tablespoons oyster sauce
100 ml hoi sin sauce
3 litres white chicken stock
  (see page 224)
2 tablespoons crushed rock sugar

Soak the wood fungus in water until they swell completely, which may
take an hour or so. (It is one of the last ingredients used.)

Rub the salt on the hocks and let them stand for at least 4 hours, then rinse.

Put hocks in a large pot and cover with cold water. Add the spring onion and the two slices of ginger then bring to the boil and simmer for 30 minutes. Strain. The hocks are three-quarters cooked by this stage, and some of the fat has been removed. In particular, the hock is moistened by the gelatine it contains, but this is left in the stock so that the final effect is not 'gummy'.

Rub dark soy sauce and ginger and spring onion juice on the pork hocks, and allow to cool.

Pat hocks dry. Place in cold oil and bring to the boil very slowly. Beware of spitting—don't stand too close! Deep-fry the hocks until crisp. (Deep-frying helps the oil penetrate the meat and loosen the tissue, preparing it for cooking. Alternatively, brush the hocks with oil and roast in a very hot oven until the skins are crispy.)

Soak the hocks in cold water for 30 minutes to replace the lost moisture. Drain well.

Heat the sesame oil and extra peanut oil in a pot and add star anise, chopped spring onion, garlic and ginger and fry until fragrant. Then add the tahini, red bean curd and brown bean paste and fry for 1 minute. Next add the light soy sauce, rice wine, vinegar chilli sauce and oyster sauce. Add the pork hocks, hoi sin sauce and just enough chicken stock to cover, then add the soaked wood fungus and rock sugar and simmer for 45 minutes.

Composition

Place each pork hock on large individual plates and place two wood fungus per hock alongside. Spoon cooking liquid over the hocks. Serve with Chinese greens and shallow-fried potatoes.

Steamed bouillabaisse custard in saffron fish consommé with fennel purée

Since my youth, I have enjoyed egg custard steamed with meats, such as the lambs' brains dish in the Neddy's chapter. Several notions went into the creation of this dish: there was the inspiration of Japanese savoury custards known as chawan mushi, using a variety of Australian fish. Then there was the French bouillabaisse, and the idea of combining this with custard. I had heard of bouillabaisse being prepared in glass, and in a terrine set with a jelly, so why not a Japanese-style bouillabaisse dish?

This is the most delicate and fragile of dishes. Its metaphor is the mosquito landing on still water—a study in surface tension. It looks as if it should break, but resists. Aim to have it just set but able to hold together.

Saffron and stock fragrance characterise this very rich bouillabaisse. By incorporating the bouillabaisse into the custard mixture, then adding a further layer of bouillabaisse over the set custard, one is able to achieve a new dimension in the enjoyment of bouillabaisse. Floating broth on top of a custard containing small treasures of seafood, served with fresh oysters, is very seductive. Serve in a chawan mushi bowl or Chinese rice bowl and on a square plate serve 2 croutons rubbed with garlic and topped with a small portion of fennel purée. Make sure that you infuse rather than boil the saffron to retain maximum fragrance.

Custard

peel of ¼ lemon
5 scallops
1 whole blue crab, fresh, including
   legs
3 red mullet fillets, halved
3 whiting fillets, halved
½ fennel bulb, sliced
4 eggs
750 ml fish stock
   (see page 221)
pinch of sea salt
pinch of freshly ground
   black pepper

Pernod or Ricard
6 leaves mitsuma
   (Japanese greens)
1 tomato, coarsely chopped
   and seeded
4 stalks parsley
½ teaspoon saffron strands
1 litre saffron fish consommé
   (see page 104)
6 fresh oysters

Fennel purée

¼ fennel bulb, sliced, reserved
   from above
olive oil

fish stock
lemon juice

Custard

Trim the pith from the lemon peel, leaving about 1 mm thickness, then blanch to remove bitterness and cut into fine 'angel hair' strands.

Plunge the scallops in boiling water then remove at once and refresh in iced water. Remove crab meat from body and legs. Trim and bone the mullet and the whiting fillets, blanch each fillet separately and quickly, then plunge in iced water. Cook fennel in salted water for 10 minutes then plunge in cold water.

Beat the eggs well with the cold stock, sea salt, pepper and Pernod. Pass through a fine sieve. Divide the lemon strands, scallops, crab meat, mullet and whiting and half the fennel amongst the bowls. Pour the egg mixture into the bowls until three-quarters full, then scrape the bubbles from the top. Put a mitsuma leaf on top of the custard in each bowl before putting them in a Chinese steamer; cover and steam for 12 minutes. Place chopped tomato, parsley and saffron in a fine sieve. Heat the consommé and slowly strain through the fine sieve, allowing the flavour from the tomato and herbs to infuse the consommé.

Fennel purée

Sauté the fennel in a little olive oil moistened with a little fish stock and a dash of lemon juice until tender. Vitamise or pass through a sieve.

Composition

Ladle fish consommé over the custard, pouring it over an inverted spoon at the edge of the bowl, in order to break the force of the consommé. Garnish with fennel purée on croutons topped with a fresh oyster, served on a separate plate.

Veal cutlet with shrimp and green tea

This dish reminds me of a Chinese temple, where the scents are always mysterious. The tea exudes freshness. When green tea is cooked it has a fishy flavour, originating from the tannin. The Chinese would call it the ultimate, 'unrecognisable on earth and made for heaven'. I first experienced Lung jian tea with shrimp in Hangchow. The shrimps, deveined and served with fresh green tea leaves on top, are no bigger than ten cent coins when they are cooked. The best veal is a very pale pink.

If you happen to live in a tea-growing area you could use the fresh green tea shoots as a substitute for the Lung jian tea. You could also garnish the dish with freshly fried young tea leaves instead of leaving them green. When you cook veal, treat it very much as you would pork. You need to seal and cook it slowly, ensuring that it does not dry out. Both veal and pork should always be served just cooked, but never underdone, so the cook must judge the timing very precisely. Slight rosiness in the very centre of the veal is acceptable to preserve the succulence, but it should never be bloody. The cucumber acts as an important third dimension in this dish. It behaves as a catalyst, melding the veal and shrimp flavours. It also provides a vegetable balance to the plate.

1 continental cucumber
6 veal cutlets, approx. 200 g each
salt
freshly ground black pepper
2 tablespoons butter
1 teaspoon Lung jian tea leaves
50 ml hot water
40 ml oil
2 shallots, finely chopped

1 clove garlic, finely chopped
30 ml rice wine, or dry white wine
120 g shrimps
20 ml ginger juice
1 teaspoon sugar
100 ml brown chicken stock
  (see page 223)
350 ml crème fraîche, whipped

Cut the cucumber into tiny barrel shapes and freeze until rock hard; this brings out the best flavour.

Season the cutlets with salt and pepper. In a large frying-pan heat the butter until very hot. Reduce to a moderate heat and seal and cook for 5 minutes on both sides. Place on a plate, cover with foil and keep warm.

Infuse the tea leaves in the hot water.

In another frying-pan heat the oil and sauté the shallots and garlic. Add in cucumber barrels, rice wine and shrimps and season with salt, ginger juice and sugar. Sauté the mixture for a few minutes then add the green tea leaves and hot water. Simmer for 2 minutes over moderate heat.

Deglaze the meat frying-pan with the chicken stock and reduce by two-thirds. Add in whipped crème fraîche and bring to the boil. Whisk then serve.

Composition

 Place the cutlets on each plate. Ladle cucumber and shrimp mixture over the cutlets and pour over the sauce.

Saltwater duck on Chinese cabbage with watercress sauce

I learnt the rudiments of this dish during the trip to Nanjing. It could easily be served with the Nanjing Salad. Created for Seppelts Menu of the Year 1992, I was determined to include a dish that was distinctly Asian, as most of the other dishes were very European. At the same time, I acknowledge that this duck dish resembles the French confit of duck, showing that greatness can derive from very different cultures, and yet be very similar. Not surprisingly then, both saltwater duck and confit of duck are held in high esteem by their respective cultures. Deciding which dishes would be included in the menu meant some tense moments. We all had our favourites—this one, fortunately, was put in; others bit the dust. There was drama, heat and light in the process. The team—Urs Inauen, Maggie Beer, Tom Milligan, food writer Nigel Hopkins as team manager, and I agreed at the very start that if we were in, then we were in it to win. We strove to avoid personal preferences and if we had to, we took a vote. Master chefs are strong individuals so working together required discipline and cooperation. It worked. We went to The Peninsula New York Hotel to repeat the menu to a demanding Big Apple audience. There are no holds barred in New York—if they don't like it, they say so! It was nerve-racking cooking there, but we needn't have worried—the event was regarded as an Australian coup. New York food writer Gail Green commented that the duck dish convinced her that we should be the winners. The dish is very demanding and not one that I undertake lightly. It needs time and finesse.

Saltwater refers to method not variety! The duck is lightly cured for three days and then cooked in a white master stock, the duck absorbing the fragrance of spice and herbs. The method of submerging, poaching and cooling the ducks, and of boiling, cooling, skimming and reheating the stock looks tedious but is essential. Once mastered, this is a technique that can be applied to other dishes. After the ducks are removed the stock is boiled again and simmered to ensure the blood is removed, leaving a clear base. Traditionally, the duck is poached for a longer time; this meat is slightly rare and therefore more 'modern European' in style. Cook the white master stock at least two hours in advance to allow the flavour of the spices to permeate the stock.

White master stock

6 star anise, whole	5 teaspoons Sichuan pepper
3 cinnamon sticks	20 pieces dried licorice root
5 teaspoons cumin seeds	2 spring onions
8 knobs ginger, bruised	100 g rock sugar
6 pieces dried tangerine peel	

Duck

2 ducks, about 2 kg each	1 litre peanut oil
1 tablespoon prickly ash per kg duck	

Chinese cabbage

1 large Chinese cabbage	1 litre brown chicken stock (see page 223)

Watercress and consommé sauce

180 ml chicken jus (see page 224)	1 teaspoon watercress, leaves only (finely sliced at last minute) freshly ground black pepper

White master stock

In 5 litres boiling water, combine all ingredients, leaving the sugar until last. Bring to the boil again and simmer for 30 minutes.

Duck

Warm the prickly ash and rub it into the duck cavities and skin. Let them stand in the fridge for at least 3 days. Submerge the ducks in cold water for an hour to remove the saltiness of the prickly ash. Blanch in boiling water then refresh in cold water.

Put ducks in the white master stock, bring to the boil then turn off the heat, steeping the ducks for at least 25 minutes. Keep tightly covered during the steeping stage. Remove ducks from the stock and allow birds to cool down. Meanwhile, bring the stock back to the boil and skim any impurities off the surface, then allow the stock to cool. After an hour, submerge the ducks in the cool stock and leave there for 4–6 hours. This final step replaces moisture and flavour. Remove the breasts from the ducks first then remove the skin from the breast. Reserve the legs for another use. Remove as much fat from the skin as possible, then cut the skin into strips. Deep-fry until crispy and use as a garnish.

Chinese cabbage

Cut the wings away from each leaf and keep the stalk only. Dismantle cabbage in this way leaf by leaf and retain the leaves. Heat the oil and deep-fry the stalks whole over a medium heat. Rinse in hot water to remove the oil.

Preheat the oven to 120°C. Place the stalks in a shallow baking dish and cover with chicken stock. Cover the dish with aluminium foil and cook in the oven for 20 minutes. Once cool, lay the stalks on a sheet of foil 30 cm x 12 cm, leaving 4 cm at either end. Lay the leaves over the stalks, roll up the foil and seal at both ends to form a cabbage roulade. Chill until firm. Once chilled, cut the roulade into 1 cm thick slices and place on a baking tray. Just before serving, warm through by placing in an oven at about 160°C for 10 minutes.

Watercress and consommé sauce

Heat the jus, add in watercress leaves and season with black pepper.

Composition

Fan the duck breast slices over the cabbage roulade on individual plates. Warm in the oven for a few minutes and serve with the watercress and consommé sauce, poured around the duck and cabbage.

Vacherin gâteau with mango sorbet and fromage blanc, served with warm chocolate tart

This dessert was inspired by Urs Inauen's raspberry sorbet and vanilla ice-cream gâteau. He maintains that this is the very best dessert for Christmas in Australia. I decided to use a tropical fruit with Kervella's white goat cheese, which has a very clean and delicate tang making it ideal for desserts. Urs came up with the poppyseeds for their slightly sweet nutty flavour. The colour scheme is great—orange and white with flecks of black.

The mango goes well with the fromage blanc: it resembles an ice-cream more than a sorbet—a richer dish for Christmas. The Kervella cheese is made in Western Australia and named after its creator. She uses milk from her own goats, which drink only spring water. This is the secret of this rich but very fresh flavoured cheese. Make the vacherin and tart pastry the day before, blind bake and store in the fridge. Use an ice-cream machine or the standard method of freezing and vitamising.

Vacherin
120 ml water
700 g sugar

12 eggwhites
juice of 1 lemon

Mango sorbet
3 large mangoes, peeled,
  chopped and puréed
juice of 1 lemon

100 g pure icing sugar
  (no added cornflour)

Fromage blanc
1 tablespoon poppyseeds
250 g Kervella fromage blanc
2 tablespoons pure icing sugar

juice of 1 lemon
1 teaspoon lemon zest, blanched
200 ml mineral water

Warm chocolate tart
180 g sweet-crust pastry
  (see page 231)
150 g bitter chocolate
  (couverture or Lindt)
1½ tablespoons sugar

1 whole egg
2 egg yolks
100 g unsalted butter, melted
thickened cream

Vacherin

Preheat the oven to 120°C. Cook the water and sugar over a medium heat until a drop of syrup added to cold water forms a soft ball. Whip the eggwhites to soft peaks and add the lemon juice. Beat further until stiff. Add the sugar syrup slowly to the eggwhites and beat to stiff peaks again. Put the meringue mixture in a piping bag with a 1 cm nozzle and pipe into two 10 cm diameter discs 2 cm thick. Bake in the oven until dry and crisp.

Mango sorbet

Sieve the mango purée and add the lemon juice. Add the icing sugar and churn in an ice-cream machine. (Alternatively, freeze and then vitamise.)

Fromage blanc

Using a mortar and pestle, grind the poppyseeds first to bring out the sweetness. Blend the fromage blanc, sugar, lemon juice, zest and mineral water together. Churn it in the ice-cream machine and mix in the poppy-seeds.

Warm chocolate tart

Preheat the oven to 180°C. Roll out the pastry to about 3 cm thickness and line six 4 cm diameter tart tins. Prick the bases with a fork and blind bake for about 10 minutes then remove the pulses and continue to bake for a further 5 minutes. Turn the oven down to 150°C. Melt the chocolate in a double boiler. Combine the sugar and the egg and egg yolks to 'ribbon' stage (when it coats a spoon), then beat in the chocolate and slowly add a stream of melted butter. Pour into the tart flans and chill for 30 minutes before baking in the oven until the chocolate filling is firm but soft in the centre.

Composition

Using one of the vacherin discs as a base, ladle stiff mango sorbet to a thickness of 3 cm over the vacherin. Put it in the freezer and chill until firm. Spoon fromage blanc on top of the sorbet and place the second vacherin disc on the top. Put them back into the freezer to chill until firm again, at least 12 hours. When ready to use, whip some cream and cover the gâteau completely with it.

Slice the gâteau into 8–10 slices. Serve with the individual warm chocolate tarts and whipped cream.

Iced fruit soup with hot ginger date pudding and coconut sorbet

If any of your guests normally avoid desserts, tempt them with the tropical fruit soup served on its own.

A fruit soup to finish off a meal is very refreshing, especially on a hot day. If you were in Asia, you would serve this with shaved ice. Some of the great French chefs also serve a fruit soup combination. As the recipes in this chapter tend to be rich, a light touch for the finale seems the right choice. Hot date and ginger pudding together with the cold soup and chilled coconut sorbet is a delectable combination. Use any fruits available—paw paw instead of sour sop for example.

Syrup
1 sour sop
1 litre mineral water
1 stick cinnamon, 2.5 cm long
1 vanilla pod
1 clove

2 sprigs mint
zest and juice of 1 lemon
zest and juice of 1 lime
100 g castor sugar

Fruit soup
6 rambutan
2 jackfruit
1 mango
2 kiwi fruit

extra kiwi fruit, pineapple,
    strawberries and banana
    for garnish

Hot date and ginger pudding
180 g fresh dates, roughly chopped
30 ml muscat
small knob ginger, grated
½ tablespoon ginger juice
180 g plain flour
250 g unsalted butter

2 whole eggs
150 g sugar
1 generous teaspoon baking soda
pinch of salt
1 vanilla pod

Coconut sorbet
150 g sugar
150 ml water
250 ml milk

500 ml coconut milk, preferably
    fresh
2 teaspoons rum

Syrup

Scrape the pulp and seeds from the sour sop and place in a pan with the mineral water. Add the cinnamon, vanilla pod and clove and bring to the boil. Simmer. Add mint, lemon and lime zest and juice to the syrup and cook for 7 minutes. Strain through a coarse sieve. Allow to cool then add in the sugar. Chill.

Fruit soup

Peel and cut the fruits into 3 cm thick pieces. Add to the syrup.

Hot date and ginger pudding

Preheat the oven to 180°C. Macerate the dates in muscat for 30 minutes. Mix the remaining ingredients together. Discard the liquid from the dates and add the dates to the mixture. Pour the mixture into dariole moulds to the top. Bake for 15 minutes. Plan to serve them warm.

Coconut sorbet

Heat the sugar and water until a drop of syrup added to cold water forms a soft ball.

Warm milk and coconut milk gently and allow to cool. Add the sugar syrup and rum. Put the mixture into an ice-cream machine. If this is not available pour the mixture into an icecube tray and freeze until solid. Blend in a vitamiser before using.

Composition

Spoon chilled tropical fruit soup into individual chilled bowls. Arrange slices of kiwi fruit, pineapple, strawberries and banana around the bowl. Spoon coconut sorbet into the centre and serve the warm pudding on a side dish.

Marjolaine

*This favourite dessert was developed by the great French chef
Fernand Point at the Pyramid Restaurant, and is a reminder of days
at Neddy's. When Mary and I bought* Great Chefs of France *she found
a marjolaine recipe and decided to try it. The butter cream in this
recipe used only butter and cream. While we were able to make a
smooth butter cream with those two ingredients, we found it very
fatty and decided to substitute a classical French butter cream using
cooked sugar and egg. The result was rewarding. It really is not
worth preparing this dessert for a small dinner party. Save it for a
gala occasion where you will need around 24 slices for your guests.*

Pastry
180 g whole unpeeled almonds
120 g hazelnuts
1¼ tablespoons plain flour

8 eggwhites
250 g sugar

Chocolate cream
200 ml crème fraîche
300 g bitter couverture, chopped

Vanilla butter cream
3 vanilla pods
1.5 kg granulated sugar
350 ml water

10 whole eggs
2 egg yolks
1.5 kg unsalted butter, softened

Praline butter spread
100 g hazelnut praline powder
100 g almond praline powder
  (or use praline paste or nougat)

1 kg vanilla butter cream
  (see above)

Garnish
chocolate shavings

icing sugar

Pastry

Preheat the oven to 160°C. Blanch and peel the almonds, then roast the almonds and hazelnuts in the oven until light brown. Grind the nuts finely in a food processor, add the flour and pass the mixture through a coarse sieve.

Beat eggwhites with 200 g of the sugar until soft peaks form. Add the remaining sugar and beat until stiff. Fold in the nut mixture carefully. Spread onto a sheet of baking paper until the mixture is about 4 mm thick. Bake for approximately 35–40 minutes.

Trim the biscuit into 4 even-sized strips. Dry out in a very low oven.

Chocolate cream

Bring the crème fraîche to the boil and cool slightly. Add the couverture and stir until smooth. Make extra if you want to cover the whole torte with the chocolate cream.

Vanilla butter cream

Scrape the vanilla seeds into the sugar and discard the pod shells. Add the water and cook the mixture until a little dropped into cold water forms a soft ball. Place the whole eggs and egg yolks in a mixer. Turn to high speed and pour in the cooked sugar mixture. Whisk until cool. Then add the butter a little at a time.

Praline butter spread

Mix the praline powders and fold into the butter cream.

Composition

Build up the cake by layering pastry, chocolate cream, pastry, butter cream, pastry and praline spread, then finish with the pastry. Either finish the marjolaine with whipped cream or cover the whole torte with chocolate cream. Divide into 24 slices. Smooth the sides, cover them with chocolate shavings and sprinkle icing sugar on top.

Favourite Desserts

My interest in desserts came late in my life as a chef; it is the area where others, starting with partner Mary Ziukelis, have most strongly influenced my thinking and finally my repertoire. This chapter is a tribute to colleagues.

During the Neddy's period I saw desserts as demanding a huge amount of patience and skill, not to mention time. Mary had all the skills to be the dessert chef at Neddy's. Her flair in this area allowed me to concentrate on the other elements of the menu.

Lenôtre, the French king of pâtisserie, claims that you must learn pâtisserie first to be a truly accomplished chef. Organisation, precision, detail, technique, specialisation, wisdom and patience are the legacy. At the Regency Hotel School I have been able to rub shoulders with master pâtissiers such as Ingo Schwarz and Hardy Jeche and highly regarded chefs such as Urs Inauen, Jean Gillard and Glen Dentice. Most of these recipes I have learned from my colleagues and they are a tribute to their skills.

This selection appeals to my Chinese palate. There is texture, colour and contrasting tastes—the attraction of these characteristics is almost genetic.

These desserts rely on the finest Australian ingredients. If you manage to get cream and butter direct from a local dairy your creations will be all the better. Eggs, too, are an important basic ingredient; buy them very fresh and use at room temperature. King Island, a small windswept green island off Tasmania, has dairy herds renowned throughout Australia for their cream and milk products. Recently, Kangaroo Island in South Australia has begun to market a cream to rival King Island's, so the new standard is encouraging competition and strengthening regional excellence. Locally made mascarpone has really taken off in the last few years and is generally very good, as are many other Australian cheeses. Whatever the credibility of the brand, it is essential to taste the cheese you wish to buy, before you buy it. This is a new industry that is still in its development phase.

Australia's standards in dessert-making are soaring, with the benefit of visiting and resident pâtissiers from Europe who have inherited generations of experience. This influence in teaching schools is now bearing fruit in the restaurant kitchens of Australia, but with a distinctive innovative overlay. Dates and saffron; cardamom and rosewater; lavender, sage and scented geranium; palm sugar and coconut milk; star fruit and pomelo; mangoes and fresh lychees; jackfruit and ginger; black rice and mung beans and our own indigenous wattleseed and rosella flowers are among the tropical and exotic ingredients and flavours found on Australian dessert menus today.

Favourite Desserts recipes

Pear and rice tart with vanilla crème anglaise

Blue-vein cheesecake with pickled cherries

Tira mi su with rhubarb sorbet

Kirsch bavarois with nectarine compôte

Lemon and lime tart

Christmas pudding

Pear and rice tart with vanilla crème anglaise

I really enjoy the nostalgia of rice cooked with milk. Adding lavender sage is a throwback to Ibiza in Spain. Mary and I visited her sister Ruta there in 1991. She introduced me to frigola, an aromatic wild thyme found throughout the island, and used in desserts and liqueurs. Lavender sage was flourishing in our back garden, and reminded me of frigola. I combined this flavour with the classic and soothing ingredients that comprise this dish to extend its horizons and offer a subtle surprise to the tastebuds. This dish was introduced to me by Glen Dentice, now at Nelson's in New Zealand.

225 g sweet-crust pastry
  (see page 231)
1 egg yolk
100 g short-grain rice
2½ tablespoons sugar
600 ml milk
4 leaves lavender sage, finely
  shredded

1 vanilla pod, split and seeded
  (retain seeds)
80 ml double cream
4 pears, poached
50 g castor sugar
2½ tablespoons butter, softened
Vanilla crème anglaise
  (see page 232)

Garnish
mint, finely shredded

Preheat the oven to 200°C. Line a 22 cm flan tin with the pastry, approximately 3 mm thick, pressing evenly into the flutes. Prick with a fork and refrigerate for 30 minutes. Blind bake for 10 minutes.

Remove the foil and pulses and return the flans to the oven for another 5 minutes. Remove again, brush with the egg yolk and return to the oven for a final 5 minutes. Remove and leave to cool.

Put the rice, sugar, milk, lavender sage and vanilla pod and seeds in a saucepan. Cover and cook gently for approximately 45 minutes, stirring from time to time to prevent the rice from sticking. Once all the milk has been absorbed, the rice should be cooked. Remove the vanilla pod and stir in the cream. Cover and leave in a warm place.

Drain the pears thoroughly, slice thinly, and arrange them in the base of the tart shell. Carefully spoon in the warm rice, bringing it right up to the level of the pastry edge. Smooth the surface with a palette knife.

Sprinkle the tart evenly with castor sugar and dot with butter then cover the pastry edge with foil to protect it. Cook under the grill until the sugar and butter are browned to a deep caramel, being careful not to let it get too dark, or the flavour will be bitter.

Remove from the grill and leave to cool to room temperature.

Composition

 Cut into slices and serve with rich vanilla crème anglaise. Garnish with finely shredded mint.

Blue-vein cheesecake with pickled cherries

Beautifully simple, this dessert was inspired by chef Urs Inauen who has developed savoury desserts as part of his repertoire. The best cheese is Richard Thomas's Meredith blue. Richard Thomas has been a pioneer of farmhouse cheeses in Australia and a consultant to various cheese producers including King Island, Milawa and Meredith. He is currently developing a new cheese house in the Yarra Valley. His cheeses are highly respected throughout Australia and he belongs to a select group of people who have developed the raw materials for quality cuisine in Australia. The pickled cherries should be stored for three weeks before serving.

Pickled Cherries
200 g castor sugar
700 ml rice vinegar

1 kg cherries, stones removed
200 ml cassise

Cheesecake
250 g sweet-crust pastry
  (see page 231)
450 g quark cheese (choose
  European-style)

150 g sugar
8 eggs
300 g Meredith blue cheese
pickled cherries or plums

Pickled Cherries

Mix the castor sugar with the rice vinegar until completely dissolved. Add the cherries and cassise and store for at least 3 weeks before serving.

Cheesecake

Preheat the oven to 180°C. Roll out the pastry and line the bottom and sides of 6 small cake rings. Blind bake for 20 minutes.

Cream the quark and sugar. Slowly add the eggs then mix in the crumbled blue cheese until it is fairly well incorporated. Pour the mixture into the pastry shells and bake for 6–7 minutes until puffed.

Composition

Serve on individual plates with either pickled cherries or plums.

Tira mi su with rhubarb sorbet

This dessert was featured in the 1990 Seppelts Menu of the Year. The final decision on the presentation came very late in the piece. A promising young pastry chef at the Hyatt, James Fenn, suggested cutting the tira mi su into a perfect diamond shape and dusting it with cocoa powder. Thin slices of rhubarb compôte, like petals, were carefully placed alongside the tira mi su.

The sensuous rhubarb sorbet, the cherry blossom imagery, and the rich flavour of the tira mi su are reminiscent of Asia, and yet you would not find such a romantic composition there.

If you do not have an ice-cream machine to make the sorbet, a serve of rhubarb compôte with a slice of tira mi su will work just as well.

Filling
120 g castor sugar
6 egg yolks
1 tablespoon custard powder
700 ml milk

7 gelatine leaves
100 g mascarpone cheese
juice and zest of ½ orange
30 ml fresh cream, lightly whipped

Syrup
200 ml water
25 ml stock syrup
  (see page 232)

25 ml Cognac
3 tablespoons coffee powder

Tira mi su
coffee almond biscuits
  (add 2 tablespoons coffee to
  Marjolaine pastry recipe on
  page 199)

chantilly cream (sweetened
  whipped cream with vanilla)
shaved chocolate

Rhubarb sorbet
400 g rhubarb
250 g castor sugar
zest of ½ orange

20 mint leaves, finely shredded
1 litre stock syrup (see page 232)
200 g Italian meringue

Filling

To make a custard, beat together the sugar, egg yolks and custard powder. In a saucepan, bring the milk to the boil then pour it over the egg mixture. Return everything to the saucepan and place it over a low flame and stir until it thickens.

Add the gelatine leaves to the hot custard then allow to cool until it is warm. Blend the mascarpone cheese with the orange juice and zest, then combine with the custard. Fold the cream into the custard mixture.

Syrup

Combine all ingredients in a saucepan over a medium heat.

Tira mi su

Line a 10 cm cake ring with plastic wrap (at least 4 cm higher than the rim of the tin) then layer the base with coffee almond biscuits to a height of 1 cm. Soak with some of the syrup. Continue to layer filling and the biscuits, soaking the biscuits each time with some syrup, finishing with biscuits. Finally, mask with chantilly cream and coat with shaved chocolate. Refrigerate for at least 1 hour, or overnight if possible.

Rhubarb sorbet

Peel and dice the rhubarb, reserving the skin. Melt the castor sugar slowly over a medium heat until it begins to caramelise. Add the rhubarb skin and cook until liquid has exuded. Remove the skin. Add the diced rhubarb to the liquid, then set aside immediately so it is not overcooked. Remove the rhubarb, add the orange zest, and reduce the remaining cooking liquid back to a syrup, then add the rhubarb again. Set aside half the diced rhubarb for a compôte and purée the remainder. Add the mint leaves to the rhubarb compôte.

Add the stock syrup to an ice-cream machine, then add in the puréed rhubarb. Just as ice crystals begin to form, add the Italian meringue.

Composition

Lift the chilled tira mi su torte from the cake ring and remove the plastic wrap. Slice into wedges. Serve on individual plates with a tablespoon each of compôte and sorbet. Spoon a little liquid from the compôte over the rhubarb.

Kirsch bavarois with nectarine compôte

This is one of my very favourite desserts, taught to me by Urs Inauen. When we started a class together at Regency Hotel School, making a bavarois as light as this was one of the most exacting feats we set our students. Light and creamy, firm but not stiff, buoyant in texture— these were the characteristics we were looking for. The combination of lime and ginger in the sauce brings out all the flavours of the dish, adding a tropical and exotic side to a classic European experience. Allow 4–5 hours' preparation time.

Bavarois
1 tablespoon almond oil
1 vanilla pod
250 ml milk
4 egg yolks
100 g castor sugar

4 leaves gelatine, soaked in
   100 ml water
300 g thickened cream
20 ml Kirsch

Nectarine compôte
6 nectarines (or other fruit)
juice of 1 lemon

juice of 1 orange
30 g castor sugar

Lime and ginger sauce
40 g castor sugar
40 ml mineral water
100 ml Grand Marnier
45 g honey
1 knob fresh ginger, finely
   shredded

zest of ½ lime, blanched, finely
   shredded
zest of ½ orange, blanched,
   finely shredded

Bavarois

Oil 6 dariole moulds or coffee cups with almond oil and chill in the refrigerator. Scrape the seeds out of the vanilla pod and add both seeds and pod to the milk. Bring to the boil in a saucepan and let it rest for 15 minutes. Beat the egg yolks and sugar until frothy and pale. Pour the milk into the yolks, a little at a time, whisking constantly.

Leave in the bowl and heat over a water bath and cook until the mixture coats the back of a spoon. Add the soaked gelatine, stir well and strain.

Allow to cool.

Whip the cream into soft peaks, but not until it is stiff. Once the mixture has completely cooled down, fold in the cream and flavour with the Kirsch. Pour the mixture into the chilled moulds and refrigerate for 4–5 hours before unmoulding.

Nectarine compôte

Blanch the nectarines, peel and slice. Bring the lemon and orange juice and sugar to the boil, reduce the heat and poach the nectarine slices for 5–10 minutes. Baste the fruit with the juices from time to time very gently, then set aside in a warm place.

Lime and ginger sauce

Melt the sugar with the mineral water until caramelised. Add the Grand Marnier and honey and reduce to a third. Add the ginger and let it sit for 10 minutes on the side of the stove. Strain and add the zest.

Composition

 Place the bavarois just off the centre of each plate. Arrange the hot compôte in front of the bavarois. Pour the lime and ginger sauce over the bavarois and serve at once.

Lemon and lime tart

Glen Dentice developed this dessert using the irresistible partnership of tangy lemon and lime. As an alternative topping, make a caramel toffee and crush it into a powder. Sprinkle this over the top of the tart and place under the griller until the toffee melts.

Sugar pastry
juice and zest of 2 lemons
125 g unsalted butter
1 vanilla pod, seeds only

100 g icing sugar
250 g plain flour
1 egg, beaten

Custard
9 whole eggs
400 g castor sugar
juice and zest of 2 limes

juice and zest of 3 lemons
250 ml King Island double cream
icing sugar

Sugar pastry

Preheat the oven to 180°C. Finely chop and double blanch the lemon zest. Rub the butter, vanilla seeds, sugar and flour together to the fine grain stage. Add the zest then the lemon juice and egg until a dough is formed, but don't overwork it. Cover and rest the dough for 45 minutes in the fridge. Roll it out until it is approximately 4 mm thick and line a tart tin. Blind bake for 20 minutes.

Custard

Reduce the oven to 120°C. Place the eggs and castor sugar in a bowl and beat with a mixer until pale and creamy. Finely chop the lime and lemon zest and double blanch. Add the lime and lemon juice and zest to the egg mixture and continue mixing. Beat the cream into soft peaks and fold into the egg mixture. Pour into the hot pastry case and return to the oven to finish cooking for around 30 minutes.

The tart must be made fresh on the day and once cooked, should be kept at room temperature. Do not chill.

Composition

Before serving, dredge the top of the tart with icing sugar and place under a griller until caramelised. Cut into slices and serve plain.

Christmas pudding

Hardy Jeche is a master pâtissier at the Regency Hotel School and when I was working out my Christmas menu for 1994 I asked if he had a recipe for a really stunning Christmas pudding. It turned out so well that I have included it here for all those who still enjoy a little British tradition at Christmas. You could macerate the fruits in grappa instead of brandy for a different taste experience. The mixture is divided in this recipe to create 20 small puddings, but, Liz has successfully made it as a single, large pudding. Make the garnish, and the puddings if you can, at least 1 month in advance.

Group 1

200 g seedless raisins
200 g sultanas
70 g candied peel
60 g glace cherries
60 g glace ginger
125 g fresh Mejghul dates
125 g glace apricots

½ Granny Smith apple, grated
½ large carrot, grated
½ small bottle Cooper's Stout
20 ml Cognac
juice of 1 orange
juice of ¼ lemon

Group 2

125 g beef suet
1 tablespoon molasses
125 g white breadcrumbs
zest of 3 oranges
zest of ½ lemon

125 g plain flour
½ teaspoon mixed spice
½ teaspoon cinnamon
½ teaspoon nutmeg
3 eggs, lightly beaten

muslin cloth
extra flour
butcher's twine

Garnish

2 cups white wine
250 g prunes
250 g apricots (Australian)

4 tablespoons brandy (or grappa)
4 tablespoons sugar
3 tablespoons dark rum

Group 1

Soak all ingredients from Group 1 overnight in a mixture of the Cooper's Stout, Cognac and citrus juices.

Group 2

Cut the beef suet into small pieces and combine with the other ingredients of Group 2.

Mix the ingredients from Group 1 and Group 2 together. Cut the muslin cloth into squares, 20 cm x 20 cm, and moisten thoroughly then generously dust with flour. Place 70 g of pudding mixture on top of the flour and wrap in the cloth. Tie with butcher's twine and cook a few at a time in a steamer over boiling water for at least 30 minutes (approximately 4 hours for 1 large pudding).

Garnish

Heat up enough white wine to cover the prunes and apricots. Bring the wine and fruit to the boil, turn off the heat and allow to stand overnight. Remove the fruit from the liquid and combine with the brandy, sugar and rum and macerate for at least 30 days or until needed.

Composition

 Serve with several pieces of macerated prunes and Australian apricots and, if you wish, a classic brandy sauce.

Master Recipes

T hese are the standard recipes used in one or more dishes in this book. They may also be useful for dishes you create yourself or adapt from other recipes.

Stocks should be fragrant and rich. Adding the herbs in the last 20 minutes gives a better result than adding them at the beginning. The herb flavours should overlay the stock, not be lost in it. You could go even further and choose to simply throw in a bouquet of freshly chopped herbs just before serving to create a distinctive fresh-flavoured stock. This is a matter of personal preference and depends on the use of the stock.

You may also want to vary the herbs. Good chefs all over the world will have their 'signature' stocks, depending on their individual tastes or what their region offers.

Cheong often uses combinations of thyme, marjoram, parsley and rosemary for game or dark meat; sage and coriander have particular uses. Citrus peel and bay leaf can add flavour but use them sparingly to avoid overpowering the dish. All the herbs used in this book are fairly standard and easy to obtain.

Preparing prawns

Prawns harvested from the sea are immediately packed in ice. The prawns absorb water from the ice, the quality of which is invariably suspect! For this reason, prawns are marinated in salt to extract this moisture. They are then rinsed under cold, running water.

salt

white rice wine

eggwhite

corn starch

peanut oil

Shell, remove heads and devein the prawns by gently pulling the innard sac from the neck of the prawns.

Add a teaspoon of salt and 1 tablespoon water to every 250 g of prawns and mix thoroughly, then rinse and drain and dry the prawns with a cloth or kitchen paper.

If the prawns are large, butterfly by cutting down the backs.

Marinate with a pinch of salt, 20 ml white rice wine and mix thoroughly until the liquid is completely absorbed by the prawns.

Then, using a coating of ½ an eggwhite, 1 teaspoon corn starch and 20 ml peanut oil, mix thoroughly. The oil helps to separate the prawns while stir frying and it also gives it a glossy look.

Plum sauce

250 g Chinese plum sauce

2½ tablespoons water

juice and rind of 4 lemons

100 g fresh plums or nectarines,
 stoned and sliced

2½ tablespoons sugar

Bring the plum sauce, water, lemon rind and fruit to the boil. Simmer for 20 minutes, then add lemon juice. Add sugar then strain the sauce and allow to cool, ready for use. To keep, place in an airtight jar and refrigerate.

Fresh tomato purée

If you can't find the fleshy, rich, ripe tomatoes that make for a good purée, then add one cup of tinned tomato purée, *not* tomato paste.

1 small onion, finely diced
3 cloves garlic, halved but
   unpeeled (the skin imparts
   a sweet flavour)
3 tablespoons olive oil
15 large ripe tomatoes, halved
   and seeded

1 tablespoon sugar
50 ml white wine (chardonnay)
1 sprig thyme
½ bay leaf
1 sprig tarragon
½ teaspoon salt
extra olive oil

In a baking tray, sauté the onion and garlic in oil. Arrange the halved tomatoes over the onions with the cut end facing down. Add the sugar and wine and cover with aluminium foil. Bake at about 160°C for 1 hour.

Remove from the oven and add in the herbs. Return to the oven, or use the stove top, and cook for a further 30 minutes. Add the salt, then pass the mixture through a fine strainer and allow to cool. Place in a container and cover with a thin film of good quality olive oil. Refrigerate and use as required.

Fish stock and farce for clarification

Use stock for moistening fish when cooking, as a base for fish soup, and for making sauces. For fish consommé, clarify the stock with the farce once the stock is cool.

Fish stock

600 g snapper bones and head
2 shallots
1 onion
1 leek, white part only
1 celery heart
5 mushrooms
¼ fennel bulb
2 cloves garlic, halved

1½ tablespoons butter
1 cup white wine (Noilly Prat)
½ lemon
5 stalks parsley
2 stalks dill
½ bay leaf
1 teaspoon sea salt
8 white peppercorns, cracked

Clean the bones and the head, remove the gills, then cut the head and bones into small pieces. Rinse thoroughly, carefully removing any clotted blood to ensure the stock is not bitter.

Peel and slice the vegetables finely. Melt the butter in a stockpot and sweat the vegetables and garlic for approximately 10 minutes over a low heat. Add the bones and sweat for a further 5 minutes until the bones are white. Add the white wine. Reduce slightly to cook off the alcohol. Cover with 1.5 litres of cold water, bring slowly to the boil, and skim off any impurities.

Peel the skin and membrane off the lemon half. Using a sharp knife, cut down one side of the membrane between each segment and flip the segment out, removing the seeds at the same time. Add the lemon, herbs and salt to the stock. Simmer for 20 minutes, skimming from time to time as required.

Add the cracked peppercorns in the last 5 minutes of the cooking process, and allow to steep for a further hour. Strain thoroughly through a fine sieve then through a muslin cloth. Chill and use immediately or freeze for later use.

Farce for clarification

500 g snapper fillet
1 large, ripe tomato
½ celery heart
½ stalk leek, white only
6 coriander roots
1 red chilli

5 mushrooms
2 cm knob fresh laos, grated
½ stalk lemon grass, chopped
1 g saffron
5 eggwhites

Chill the snapper fillet for 30 minutes then mince through a coarse mincer. Cut the tomato, celery heart, leek, coriander roots, chilli and mushrooms finely and mix in with the minced seafood. Add in the grated laos, chopped lemon grass and saffron. Lightly whisk eggwhites and fold into the other ingredients. Knead well with your hands to form a thick batter.

Stir the farce into the cool fish stock and slowly bring to the boil, skimming all impurities from the surface. Simmer for 1 hour, or until the stock is clear, and the flavour is strong. Strain the consommé through a muslin cloth and allow liquid to cool. Discard the rest.

Brown chicken stock

This stock is used for making chicken jus, and as a base for other sauces that require a meat glaze. When using it with meats other than chicken, lightly brown off the meat trimmings and add to the stock.

It can even be used for fish or lobster, to bolster a fish stock before reducing it to a glaze. This stock relies on the gelatinous parts of the chicken.

5 chicken feet
3 kg chicken bones
1 kg chicken wings
300 g celeriac
200 g carrots
400 g onions
6 parsley stalks
4 thyme sprigs
1 bay leaf

1 leek, white part only roughly
    chopped (reserve a few outer
    leaves)
500 g ripe, soft tomatoes
200 g mushrooms
6 whole bulbs garlic
300 ml oil (grapeseed or peanut)
1 teaspoon salt
1 tablespoon black peppercorns,
    crushed

Chop feet, bones and wings into walnut-sized pieces. Clean, peel and roughly chop the celeriac, carrots, leeks and onions (mirepoix). Bind the herbs in the outer leek leaves to form a bundle. Cut the tomatoes into quarters, slice the mushrooms and cut the unpeeled garlic bulbs in half.

Preheat the oven to 220°C. Heat the oil in a large pan and, once it is hot, add the chicken bones and turn them over in the oil until evenly coated. Sprinkle with salt. Return the bones to the oven and cook until light brown in colour.

Add mirepoix and garlic and continue roasting until the vegetables are lightly browned. Remove the bones, vegetables and garlic and set aside in a stock pot. Remove the fat from the roasting tray and add in the tomatoes and mushrooms. Return the tray to the oven and roast until the liquid has evaporated, taking care not to burn the vegetables.

Pour a little water or white wine into the roasting tray, scrape the residue from the bottom and add it to the stockpot with the roasted vegetables. Add enough cold water to just cover the bones and bring slowly to boil. Skim off all impurities and fat. Add the herb bundle and simmer gently for 3–4 hours, stirring from time to time. Add the crushed peppercorns in the last 30 minutes of cooking time. Strain the stock through a fine sieve, then through a muslin cloth. Chill, then, when you use the stock or freeze it, remove the fat from the top.

Chicken jus

Reduce Brown Chicken Stock to one-third (see page 223).

White chicken stock

Because is has not been exposed to dry heat, white chicken stock does not brown. It is used for general purposes, such as soups and sauces, and for dishes where colour is important, such as vegetables, rice and cream- or white-coloured sauces.

1 kg chicken bones, cut into
  walnut-size pieces
2 sticks celery
1 leek
1 onion
1 clove

1 sprig thyme
1 small bay leaf
6 parsley stalks
pinch of salt
10 white peppercorns

To remove blood and impurities, plunge the bones in boiling water. Bring the water back to the boil and remove the bones. Refresh them in cold water. Place the bones in a stockpot and cover with 3 litres of water. Bring to the boil and skim off any impurities. Simmer for 1½ hours.

Add vegetables and herbs and cook for a further 30 minutes. Ten minutes before the end of the cooking process, add the salt and the peppercorns. Strain the stock through a fine sieve, then through a muslin cloth.

Chill, then, when you are going to use the stock, or freeze it, remove any remaining fat.

Chicken fumet and farce for clarification

Chicken fumet

1 small leek, pale part only
1 large onion
2 small celery stalks, pale part only
150 g button mushrooms
2 sprigs thyme
2 sprigs parsley
1 bay leaf

4 kg chicken wings, leg bones
  and carcases
1 tablespoon butter
2 cloves garlic, crushed
20 black peppercorns, crushed
salt

Finely slice the leek, onion, celery and mushrooms. Tie up the herbs in some muslin cloth.

Chop the chicken bones into walnut-size pieces. Melt the butter in a saucepan. Sweat the bones without browning them for 5 minutes, add the vegetables, herbs, garlic and peppercorns, and sweat for a further 5 minutes.

Cover with cold water and add a little salt. Bring to the boil and simmer for 3 hours, skimming from time to time. Strain through a fine sieve. Allow to cool.

Farce for clarification

500 g chicken leg meat
1 large, ripe tomato
2 shallots
½ small leek, pale part only

½ small celery stalk, pale part only
3 button mushrooms
5 eggwhites
5 black peppercorns, crushed

Mince the chicken through a coarse mincer. Cut all the vegetables finely. In a bowl, beat the eggwhites lightly and add in the chicken, vegetables and crushed peppercorns. Knead well with your hands to form a thick batter. Stir into the chicken fumet. Bring slowly to the boil and remove the scum with a slotted spoon. Simmer for 1–1½ hours or until the consommé is clear and the flavour is strong enough. Strain though a fine sieve and then through a muslin cloth and set the resultant chicken consommé aside to cool. Discard the residue.

Brown veal stock

A versatile stock used for soups and sauces.

2 kg veal bones, knuckles if
  possible
250 g onions
100 g celeriac (or celery)
100 g carrots
200 g tomatoes
2 cloves garlic

100 g mushrooms
2 sprigs thyme
½ bay leaf
6 whole parsley stalks
100 ml peanut oil
1 tablespoon salt
6 white peppercorns, cracked

Preheat the oven to 220°C. Using a heavy cleaver, cut the bones into walnut-sized pieces or ask the butcher to do it for you. Roughly dice all the vegetables, except the mushrooms, into mirepoix, and cut each tomato into 8 sections. Peel and halve the garlic cloves. Roughly chop the mushrooms. Tie the herbs together.

Heat the oil in a roasting pan, add the bones and brown them off. Add mirepoix and garlic. Roast them in the oven until they are light brown. Add the mushrooms and roast for another 2–3 minutes, then add the tomatoes and keep roasting until all the juices have evaporated and the tomatoes have become slightly coloured.

Place everything in a stockpot, deglaze the pan with water to remove the caramelised residue from the bottom. Add the pan liquid to the stockpot and cover the bones and vegetables generously with cold water. Bring slowly to the boil.

Skim the surface thoroughly. Add the salt and herbs and simmer for approximately 5 hours. Add the peppercorns to the stock in the last 10 minutes of the cooking process. Strain stock through a fine sieve and then through a muslin cloth. Return to the boil before allowing it to cool down. Chill and remove any remaining fat before using or freezing.

Veal jus

Principally used for sauces, veal jus requires a similar method to Brown Veal Stock. In fact, you could achieve almost the same result by simply reducing the Brown Veal Stock to one-third. However, the following recipe is richer and more gelatinous.

2 kg veal knuckle bones
1 kg chicken and turkey wings
100 ml peanut oil
1 onion
3 stalks celery
2 medium-sized carrots
100 g mushrooms

3 medium ripe tomatoes
½ teaspoon salt
2 sprigs thyme
3 stalks parsley
½ bay leaf
10 black peppercorns, cracked

Preheat the oven to 220°C. Cut the meats and bones into walnut-sized pieces using a heavy cleaver, or ask the butcher to do it for you. Heat the oil in a large roasting pan and brown the bones in the oven, stirring from time to time.

Clean, peel and roughly dice the onion, celery and carrots into mirepoix. Add these vegetables to the bones, and brown lightly.

Add the mushroom and quartered tomatoes. Sweat these until all the juices have evaporated, then add a little water and loosen the residue from the bottom of the pan.

Transfer everything to a stockpot. Cover with cold water, add the salt and bring slowly to the boil, skimming well. Simmer for 5 hours, adding the herbs and pepper in the last hour. Keep skimming from time to time.

Strain well through a fine sieve and then through a muslin cloth. Chill and remove any fat before using or freezing.

Brown lamb stock

This stock is used for lamb dishes. It can also be reduced to form a lamb jus which is used in lamb and hogget dishes to enrich the sauce.

2 kg lamb bones
60 ml peanut oil
1 large onion
2 medium carrots
1 stalk celery
1 bulb garlic

3 tomatoes, chopped
½ teaspoon salt
5 stalks parsley
1 bay leaf
10 black peppercorns, cracked

Preheat the oven to 250°C. Chop the lamb bones into walnut-sized pieces, using a heavy cleaver, or ask the butcher to do it for you. Heat the oil in a deep roasting pan and add the bones, turning them over in the oil. Roast in the oven for 20–25 minutes.

Clean and peel the onion, carrots and celery then roughly dice into mire-poix. Peel the garlic and cut it in half lengthwise. Add the mirepoix and garlic to the roasting tray and roast in the oven with the bones until light brown, stirring frequently.

Add the tomato, stir and cook until all the juices have evaporated.

Transfer the bones and vegetables to a stockpot. Add water to the roast-ing tray and scrape away the residues. Pour the liquid into the stockpot.

Cover the bones completely with cold water. Add salt and slowly bring to the boil. Skim, add parsley and bay leaves. Simmer for 3 hours, skimming from time to time.

Add the cracked peppercorns 20 minutes before the end of the cooking time. Strain well through a fine sieve then through a muslin cloth. Chill and remove any fat before using or freezing.

Kangaroo stock

This stock is mainly used for making kangaroo jus to enrich sauces to accompany kangaroo dishes. Brown Veal Stock or Veal Jus can be used instead.

2 kg kangaroo bones	5 soft ripe tomatoes
1 kg kangaroo tail	4 juniper berries
80 ml olive oil	black peppercorns
50 g bacon rind	1 litre red wine
1 onion	100 ml port wine
2 carrots	1 teaspoon salt
½ celeriac	1 bay leaf
1 whole bulb garlic	6 parsley stalks
100 g mushrooms	

Preheat the oven to 220°C. Chop the bones and tail into walnut-sized pieces using a heavy cleaver or ask the butcher to do it for you. Heat the oil in a roasting pan, add the bones and bacon rind and roast until light brown.

Roughly dice the onion, carrots and celeriac into mirepoix. Halve the garlic bulb. Chop the mushrooms roughly and quarter the tomatoes. Crack the juniper berries and black peppercorns and set aside.

Add the mirepoix to the bones and keep roasting until lightly coloured. Add the mushrooms, garlic and tomatoes and roast until the juices have evaporated. Transfer the bones and vegetables to a stockpot. Remove the fat from the roasting pan, deglaze with the red wine and port wine and add to the bones.

Cover the bones with cold water then bring to the boil, stirring well. Add the salt, bay leaf and parsley stalks. Simmer for 4 hours, stirring from time to time.

Add the peppercorns and juniper berries, then simmer for a further 30–60 minutes. Strain well through a fine sieve then through a muslin cloth. Chill and remove any fat before using or freezing.

Sourdough

Sourdough requires 72 hours to stand before it can be used. It is a starter dough for Chinese buns.

1.5 kg baker's flour	*30 g salt*
1.2 litres water	*½ onion*

In a mixing bowl, mix together 300 ml water and 500 g flour, 10 g salt and the onion. Leave the mixture to stand in a warm place for 24 hours.

The following day, remove the onion and add 500 g flour, 300 ml water and 10 g salt. Cover with a damp cloth and leave in a warm place for a further 24 hours. The next day repeat the process.

Brioche

20 g fresh yeast	*10 egg yolks*
1 tablespoon milk	*10 g salt*
500 g flour	*350 g butter*

Dissolve the yeast in the milk. Using an electric mixer, mix together the flour, eggs, salt and yeast mixture then knead until the dough no longer sticks to the bowl. Cover with a damp cloth then set aside and allow it to double in size.

Once doubled, add in the butter and knead the dough until the butter has been completely incorporated. Set aside and allow to double in size once more.

Knead and break the dough into small pieces. Refrigerate for at least a day before using. Bake at 200°C for 20 minutes.

Plain noodle dough

1 tablespoon light olive oil
1½ tablespoons spring water
1 large whole egg

1 extra egg yolk
1 teaspoon salt
1 cup plain flour

Lightly whisk together olive oil, water, whole egg, egg yolk and salt. Place flour in a separate mixing bowl and make a well in the centre. Pour the lightly whisked mixture into the well. Using your fingers, slowly gather in all the flour by working from the centre of the well until it is completely incorporated. Do not add extra water as the dough should be firm. If the dough really feels too dry, sprinkle a little water on sparingly. Gather all the flour and make a log shape about 20 cm long. Cover with a damp cloth or plastic wrap and leave to rest for 2 hours before using.

Roll out the dough very thinly on your pasta machine or roll by hand into large, thin sheets. Use cornflour or rice flour when dusting, rather than plain flour. If the dough is not fine enough roll it out further by hand.

Puff pastry

500 g plain flour
200 ml iced water
pinch of salt

1½ tablespoons cider vinegar
50 g butter, melted
400 g butter, softened

Sieve the flour onto a workbench and make a well in the centre. Pour the water, salt, vinegar and melted butter into the well.

Work all the ingredients together with the fingertips of one hand. Use your other hand to push small quantities of flour into the centre, as it tends to spread out. When all the ingredients are well combined, work the dough lightly with the palm of your hand until smooth.

Form a rectangle and lightly prick the surface with a knife to break the elasticity. Wrap the dough in a polythene bag or greaseproof paper and chill in the refrigerator for 3–4 hours.

Roll the pastry into a 60 cm x 30 cm rectangle, spread the soft butter over two-thirds of the surface, fold in the third without butter then lay one of the other thirds on top. Refrigerate for 30 minutes.

Roll the dough out into a 50 cm x 30 cm rectangle. Mark the dough into 3 equal parts and fold the two end thirds onto the centre third. This is the first turn.

Turn the rectangle through 90° and roll it out gently and progressively away from you, flouring the work surface as you roll.

Once again, roll the dough into a 50 cm x 30 cm rectangle and repeat the folding process. At this stage, wrap the pastry in the polythene bag or greaseproof paper and refrigerate again for 30–60 minutes.

Remove and repeat the last 2 turns in the same way. Rest for 30 minutes.

Repeat the last 2 turns once more so that you have 6 turns. Refrigerate for at least 1 hour before using. This pastry freezes well.

Sweet-crust pastry

1 egg
1 egg yolk
100 g pure icing sugar
pinch of salt

finely grated zest of ½ lemon
125 g butter, softened
250 g plain flour

In a large bowl, mix together the whole egg, the yolk, icing sugar, salt and the lemon zest for 1 minute. Add the softened butter and mix thoroughly.

Sift in the flour and rub it in with your fingertips until the dough has a rough, sandy texture.

Press the dough together and wrap it in plastic wrap. Refrigerate for at least 2 hours before using.

Stock syrup

1 kg castor sugar   1 litre spring water

Place the water and sugar in a saucepan over a high heat, stirring with a
wooden spoon until dissolved. Continue heating until the syrup comes to
a full boil then remove the saucepan from the heat. Leave to cool
completely before use.

Vanilla crème anglaise

500 ml milk   2 vanilla beans
250 ml rich cream   6 large egg yolks
180 g castor sugar

Gently bring the milk, cream, sugar and vanilla beans to just boiling. In a
bowl, lightly whisk the egg yolks. Pour the hot milk mixture over the egg
yolks.

Heat the bowl over a water bath, stirring the mixture constantly until it
coats the back of a spoon.

Glossary

Abalone mushrooms An Asian variety with a distinctive light and mild fragrance, and a soft and succulent texture. Can be used in salads and as a vegetable. Australian markets and fine food shops stock freshly grown abalone mushrooms. Tinned supplies are also available, but the texture is not as soft.

Ammonium carbonate Available in Chinese groceries and used for steamed buns and other breads. It has a different effect from a raising agent—it 'bursts' the dough.

Asian salted fish (ham yui, or 'dried sun') Any variety of fish salted and dried in the sun (red-eyed snapper or mulloway are generally used). Available in packets from Asian grocery shops. Some are salty moist, others are very dry. Kuantan produces the most prized moist version in Malaysia.

Baking powder, double-action variety An American product used as a raising agent by the Chinese for buns, cakes and pastries. Available at Chinese groceries— generally in a distinctive red tin.

Balsamic vinegar Prized Italian aged vinegar, available in Continental food shops. The best varieties come from Modena. The 'Aceto' method is the traditional method of making it— country-style, using wooden barrels.

Bamboo shoots Can be obtained fresh, braised in tins, or dried from Asian grocery shops. The tinned Ma-Ling brand is the best. (Fresh ones require considerable knowledge to prepare properly.) There are both spring and winter varieties. Store any leftover shoots in the fridge, but cover them with water and change the water daily. Keep for no longer than five days.

Bean curd Made from soy beans; available in Asian groceries and health food shops. There are many forms—fresh soft, fresh medium, fresh hard, dried, fried, sweetened and so forth. Most recipes call for the fresh soft white bean curd. This can be stored in the fridge, covered with water. The water must be changed daily. Do not keep longer than three days. After that it can be washed and frozen and used for deep frying. To make this harder, you can blanch it, then place a weight on it for 6 hours. It is fat free, bland, nutritious, and very versatile. Appreciation of its smoothness and blandness comes with experience.

You can buy bean curd in sticks; these are made from the residue of soy bean milk and purchased in dried form. Reconstitute in warm water.

Bean curd skin pastry is similar to the sticks, but comes in large sheets, which are used to hold stuffings for deep-frying.

Bean paste *see* Brown bean paste

Beef tendon Tendon from the hind legs, cooked long enough to acquire a gelatinous texture.

Blachan A Malaysian and Indonesian word for fermented shrimp paste. It comes

in paper-wrapped blocks or jars (the latter is generally of a better quality), and keeps indefinitely. A moist block is best. To use, wrap tightly in clingfilm, two or three layers, and place in microwave on high for two or three minutes. It can then be crumbled for use in curry pastes (rempahs).

Black moss (fat choy)   This is really a fine, hairlike seaweed. The Chinese name indicates that it is rejuvenating and especially good for healthy lungs, and for its iron content.

Black salt   A mined salt with a variety of mineral content.

Brown bean paste   Caramelised, salted paste of brown (soy) beans, used extensively in Chinese dishes. Not to be confused with whole brown beans. However, if you fry the whole beans with garlic and sugar, you will achieve the same result, and probably a better one.

Cabbage see Chinese cabbage, Swamp cabbage (kangkong)

Callop   Freshwater fish found in the Murray or farmed in ponds.

Candlenuts   A nut used extensively in Asian curry dishes as a thickener and flavour enricher. It is very rich in oil and was used like a candle traditionally.

Cardamom, black   Larger and darker than the normal 'white' cardamom, this has a strong smoky, eucalypt aroma. It is used for perfuming curries.

Carrot oil   A reddish oil obtained from cooking carrot very gently for a long time in safflower, peanut or grapeseed oil.

Chilli oil   A very hot, red oil, with sesame oil as a base. Two or three drops is generally all that is required for a dish, as it is very powerful.

Chinese black (or dried) mushrooms   These are shiitake mushrooms, but once dried, the flavour is different. A cracked, thick, dried type is the one to seek out at Asian grocery shops. To reconstitute, soak in hot water for 30 minutes. The stems are usually removed.

Chinese cabbage   A long-headed cabbage, pale yellow/green in colour, wih a tightly wrapped form and large stem base. Available in Chinese groceries and many greengrocers.

Choy sum   Long green 'bone-stemmed' leafy vegetable, with a yellow flower when mature. Used very often for quick noodle dishes.

Cloud-ear fungus   A type of wood fungus, obtained in dried form. Place in hot water for 15 minutes to reconstitute. It is soft yet slightly crunchy when cooked. Has been proven to reduce blood cholestorol levels.

Coconut cream and milk   Fresh dried coconut kernels are grated and the meat is squeezed to obtain the rich 'cream'. When water has been added, it can be squeezed again to get coconut 'milk'. When using the tinned kind, just scrape off the thick part for 'cream', or shake well for 'milk'.

Crème fraîche Rich cream which has been lightly fermented, but is not sour. It has a slightly tangy, nutty flavour. There are several Australian varieties. Consult French cookbooks to prepare your own, using buttermilk.

Crumpet flour An Australian milling industry term for a low-gluten flour. Ideal for making short biscuits and light buns, including Chinese white steamed buns.

Daikon Japanese word for Chinese radish. Available in Asian groceries and some greengrocers. It is mild—quite different from European radish.

Dariole moulds Shaped like flowerpots in different sizes. Used for everything from timbales to sweet puddings.

Dried fish/whitebait Tiny dried fish used for making stock, sambal or just deep fried. Known in Malaysia as ikan belis. The Japanese packs are the best, as the fish have generally been cleaned. They must be rinsed, but not soaked, in water several times before use to remove scales.

Dried oysters Available in packets in Asian grocery shops. Reconstituted by soaking in warm water for several hours. Remove all grit. Dried oysters are supposed to increase breast milk in nursing mothers and help build up the blood.

Dried scallop paste Available in jars from Asian groceries. Contains soy sauce and chilli. This is expensive nourishing food which is used in Chinese medicinal culture to help strengthen the 'yin' of the body. If unavailable, buy dried scallops, add water and cook till soft. Use both liquid and scallops.

Eggs, preserved black *see* Preserved black eggs

Enoki mushrooms Fresh enoki mushrooms are now available in Australia—they are commercially cultivated in Melbourne.

Fish sauce Derived from fish that are packed in barrels with salt. The extract is thin, salty and brown and is used extensively in Asian dishes. Vietnamese fish sauce tastes 'fishier'.

Frisée lettuce A pale green-white variegated endive with frilled leaves. The taste is less bitter than the traditional green endive.

Fungus *see* Cloud-ear fungus, Wood fungus

Galangal A rhizome similar to ginger, this is great with fish and white meat.

Ginger, *see* Japanese pickled ginger, Pickled ginger

Ginger juice Obtained by crushing fresh ginger and squeezing out the juice.

Ginkgo nut The edible kernel of the inedible fruit of the maidenhair tree which grows in Asia and Australia. It has an individual fragrance and is used in vegetarian dishes or soups. Can be purchased in tins (never eaten raw).

Gluten balls Deep-fried pastry balls which can be purchased dry or ready to use in cans. They are soaked in water before use, and have a silky feel. Used for special vegetarian dishes.

Hoi sin sauce Made from soy beans, garlic, pumpkin, oyster extract, spices and large chillis. It can be purchased in tins or jars at Asian groceries. It has a spicy, sweet flavour and is used in Chinese dishes or as a dip for white chicken and pork. It keeps well under refrigeration with a layer of oil on top.

Japanese pickled ginger Ginger pickled in vinegar and sugar and coloured pink. Can be purchased from Asian groceries.

Jasmine tea Distinguished from other black Chinese teas by its use of jasmine flowers to scent the tea leaves. Widely available.

Jellyfish Available from Asian groceries, salted and vacuum packed. It has to be soaked for several hours in several changes of water before use.

Kaffir lime leaves A fragrant addition to Thai dishes. Each leaf looks like two leaves.

Kangkong *see* Swamp cabbage

Kaoling wine A northern-region, Chinese-style grappa with a high alcohol level, made from sorghum grass. Used extensively for Chinese roasts and other dishes.

Laos root A South-east Asian rhizome also known as greater galangal. Can be purchased in dried or powdered form, but is also available fresh in Australia from Chinese groceries and markets. It adds a special fragrance to dishes and is documented as having been used in sixteenth-century English cookery for perfuming game meat.

Lemon grass An aromatic Asian plant that is also grown in Australia and other continents. The white bulb base is the part that is generally used for curries and other aromatic dishes. It helps digestion of fatty dishes.

Licorice roots These have a sweet and fragrant effect. Obtainable in dried slices from Asian groceries and health food shops.

Lily buds Long, narrow golden buds with a very delicate flavour, used in Chinese dishes. Obtained in dry form from Chinese groceries. Reconstitute by soaking in hot water for 30 minutes. Discard the water.

Lotus root Tubers of the lotus plant, available from Chinese groceries; used as a vegetable and in desserts. The tinned variety is acceptable—use immediately after opening. We have plenty of fresh lotus roots in northern Australia. The Chinese believe that teenagers or adults who suffer from acne, skin rashes, eczema or psoriasis should drink raw lotus root juice or eat tinned lotus roots boiled with mung beans in a soup. It helps to 'cool' the blood system.

Lotus seed paste A yellowish paste that is prepared with sugar and used for buns and cakes. Obtained from Chinese groceries.

Lye water An alkaline water used in the making of noodles to strengthen the dough. It also neutralises the sour-acid content of bun dough. (Can also be used to mop the floor!) Obtainable from Chinese groceries.

Maltose This is the sugar extracted from malt. Used in Chinese 'skin' roasting. Available from Chinese groceries.

Mandoline cutter A multi-purpose cutting tool used for slicing, chopping and shredding.

Meringue, Italian Egg white whipped to a peak with hot sugar syrup at 116° C.

Mirepoix Roughly chopped vegetables, including carrots, leeks, celery and other stock vegetables, for soups.

Moss, black, see Black moss

Mushrooms see Abalone mushrooms, Chinese black mushrooms, Enoki mushrooms, Pine mushrooms, Shiitake mushrooms

Mustard greens A type of Chinese vegetable, slightly bitter in flavour.

Ong choy see Swamp cabbage.

Oyster sauce Oyster extract with salt, soya sauce and wheat starch, used in many Chinese dishes to enhance flavours. The best variety comes from Macau near Hong Kong.

Oysters, dried see Dried oysters

Palm sugar Strong-flavoured dark sugar obtained from the sap of coconut palms, essential for certain desserts and curries. Generally sold in round flat cakes. A lighter variety can be obtained in jars but this is not quite so flavoursome.

Pandan leaf An aromatic green leaf, prized in South-east Asia. Imparts a special flavour to savoury dishes and sweetmeats.

Pepper, Sichuan see Sichuan pepper

Pickled ginger Ginger lightly salted and then preserved in rice vinegar.

Pine mushrooms These are found in pine forests in winter, and are only available fresh.

Preserved black eggs Also known as 1000-year-old eggs, these have been coated in ash to prevent deterioration. The yolk shows five bands of shades of grey. Used in special Chinese dishes, especially rice porridge.

Prickly ash Ground Sichuan peppercorns toasted in a dry frying pan with salt (one part peppercorn to three parts salt).

Red bean curd A fermented soy bean curd soaked in alcohol, salt and water. Comes in red and white forms, with each having a slightly different flavour. Can be used to flavour meat dishes. Do not leave in an opened jar with a metal lid.

Red bean paste Made by cooking red beans with sugar. Like lotus seed paste, used for buns and cakes. Available in Chinese groceries.

Red dates Grown in northern China. They are available dried from Chinese

groceries. Used to sweeten stocks and are supposed to have health-giving properties, including strengthening of the legs. To prepare, soak in warm water and remove inner stone. They absorb the 'fishy' flavour when steaming fish.

Rempah Herbs and spices ground to a paste and used in curries.

Rice vinegar White: a fairly sharp vinegar used for pickling and to enhance flavours, in sweet and sour dishes. Obtainable from Chinese groceries.
Black: used principally for dipping sauces. Red: used also for dipping and for colouring skin of chicken and pork in roast dishes.

Rock sugar Crystallised sugar made from raw sugar, having a less sweet flavour than refined white sugar. To measure, crush first and place in measuring spoon.

Rose wine A Kaoliang wine to which rose fragrance is added. It is principally used in the seasoning of poultry.

Sabayon An egg emulsion of very light consistency. Whisk eggs until very frothy, then whisk further over a hot water bath, maximum 55°C, until it starts to coat the back of a wooden spoon. Consult a classic recipe book for further details.

Salt fish *see* Asian salted fish

Sat choy Small bak choy—a Chinese baby vegetable with white stems and green leaves that is very fashionable for use in salads

Sea cucumber Black, dried rock-like sea slug also known as bêche-de-mer. Available from Chinese groceries, it must be soaked for a few days in water and then simmered for one hour before cleaning.

Sesame oil Made from toasted sesame seeds, it is highly aromatic and is generally used sparingly for seasoning.

Shallot oil Made by frying fresh shallots in oil. (You can substitute the green part of spring onion and achieve a similar flavoured oil). Used to enhance flavours in Asian dishes, for example, on steamed fish or on vegetables.

Shark lips These come in long dried pieces and are light golden in colour. They must be soaked in water for a day. Any meat and sandy skin attached to the cartilage is then removed using a brush. Used in braised seafood dishes, especially for their texture and health-giving properties.

Shiitake mushrooms Fresh shiitake mushrooms can be obtained in Australian markets and fine food shops. They have a mild flavour and a meaty texture. For the dried variety, *see* Chinese dried mushrooms

Sichuan peppercorn A distinctively flavoured dark red peppercorn, more eucalyptus than peppery, used especially deep-fried or roasted meat dishes.
See also Prickly ash

Soy sauce Light: there are many varieties readily available in Chinese groceries. Used extensively as a seasoning, it can substitute for salt. One recommended brand is Pearl River Bridge from China, but make sure it is the authentic one.

Generally, look for a full bean-flavoured taste, good light caramel colour and a slightly alcoholic edge to the flavour. I prefer the Tinsong Tin label, but Japanese varieties are generally of reasonable quality. Dark: contains sugar and is especially useful for darker sauces, or for dipping where slight sweetness is required. (Not to be confused with kecap manis, an Indonesian soy, sugar and caramel sauce.

Spring onion   Juice: made by crushing the juice out of the white part. Used for seasoning and marinating meat. Paste: finely chopped whites of spring onion.

Star anise   Dried, star-shaped fruit of a tree native to China. There are eight segments to each star. Used to flavour master stocks, beef, lamb and poultry. Available from Chinese groceries and some supermarkets.

Sugar   *see* Palm sugar, Rock sugar

Swamp cabbage (kangkong)   An Asian vegetable grown in waterlogged conditions, this has a hollow stem and pointed green leaves and is available in Chinese groceries. It has a combination of a soft (leaves) and crunchy (stem) texture and is delectable for this reason. It must be cooked.

Syrup stock   Half sugar, half water brought to a boil. *See* Master Recipes

Tamarind   The fruit of a tropical tree, it has a furry brown skin and tangy acid fruit. Sold vacuum-packed in Chinese groceries and used in sweet-sour curries.

Tangerine peel, dried   Generally sun-dried, and adds fruit flavour to stews and stocks. Available in Chinese groceries.

Tapioca starch   Obtainable from Chinese groceries, it has a binding strength for particular pastries. It can be used as a thickener but it is not recommended for sauces.

Valita spinach   An English variety with pink stems.

Vinegar   *see* Balsamic vinegar, Rice vinegar

Water chestnuts   Available fresh and in tins. Found in the Kakadu region of the Northern Territory. Peel fresh ones, removing brown outer skin. Tinned (peeled) water chestnuts can be stored for three days in water—change water daily.

Wheat starch   Used for thickening and obtainable from Asian groceries. A recommended brand is Foo Yuen Loong.

White bean curd   *see* Red bean curd

Wine   Chinese wines include Kaoliang, sorghum wine made in northern China (*see* Rose wine), and yellow rice wine, an aromatic wine giving a special flavour to dishes. The best variety of yellow rice wine is Shaoshing from eastern China.

Wood fungus   For recipes with wood fungus, use the 'silverside' variety. It comes in dried form and requires longer soaking and cooking than other wood funguses. It assumes the flavour of the dish and has a distinctive crunchy texture. Used particularly in braised dishes.

Index